Instant Pot Cookbook
Ultimate Instant Pot Recipes For Smart People
(2018 Recipes)

Robin Gibbs

TERMS & CONDITIONS

No part of this cookbook should be transmitted or reproduced in any form whatsoever, including electronic, print, scanning, photocopying, recording or mechanical without the prior written permission of the author. All the information, ideas and guidelines are for educational purpose only. The writer has tried to ensure the utmost accuracy of the content provided in the book, all the readers are advised to follow instructions at their own risk. The author of this book cannot be held liable for any incidental damage, personal or even commercial caused by misrepresentation of the information given in the book. Readers are also encouraged to seek professional help when needed.

TABLE OF CONTENTS

CHAPTER 1: INTRODUCTION 1

CHAPTER 2: THE AMAZING WORLD OF INSTANT POT 2

CHAPTER 3: INSTANT POT BUTTONS 4

CHAPTER 4: HOW IT WORKS? 6

CHAPTER 5 - CLEANING TIPS 7

CHAPTER 6: INSTANT POT PRESSURE COOKING TIME CHARTS 9

CHAPTER 7: RECIPES 16

BREAKFAST 16

YUMMY BREAKFAST ESPRESSO OATMEAL 16

UNIQUE COCONUT CORNMEAL PORRIDGE 17

ULTIMATE DELICIOUS VANILLA STEEL CUT OATS 19

ICONIC SCOTCH EGGS WITH GROUND SAUSAGE 20

AWESOME HAM & EGG CASSEROLE 22

SUPER OATMEAL WITH NUTS 24

DELIGHTFUL CREAMY BANANA BREAKFAST BREAD 26

FANTASTIC CHEESE QUICHE 27

GREAT FRUITED STEEL-CUT BREAKFAST OATS 29

HAPPY STRAWBERRY CREAM OATMEAL 31

FISH AND SEAFOOD 32

FANTASTIC CREAMY COCONUT FISH CURRY 32

GREAT BUTTER SHRIMP PAELLA 34

HAPPY CALAMARI IN TOMATO SAUCE 37

LUCKY SPICY CAJUN & LIME SHRIMP (GLUTEN-FREE) 39

VINTAGE MUSSELS IN CITRUS JUICE AND DRY WHITE WINE 40

BEST FISH CURRY 42

NOSTALGIC SWEET SOY FISH 44

MIGHTY SPICY CHILI SNAPPER 46

KING SIZED MARJORAM SALMON 48

CRAZY SALMON & SPINACH PENNE 50

POULTRY AND CHICKEN **51**

YUMMY CHICKEN POT PIE 51

TASTY CLASSIC SPICED CHICKEN BREASTS 53

TITANIC TOMATO CHICKEN STEW 55

RICH CHICKEN SALSA 57

ELEGANT ORANGE SPICE CHICKEN 58

WONDERFUL CHICKEN AND POTATOES DISH 60

QUICK SPICY CHICKEN CURRY 62

AWESOME EGGPLANT THAI STYLE CHICKEN 64

LEGENDARY SHREDDED CHICKEN 66

EXCELLENT ITALIAN CHICKEN THIGHS. 68

GRAINS AND BEANS **69**

LUCKY BOILED KIDNEY BEANS 69

VINTAGE SPINACH CHICKPEA CURRY 71

BEST CREAMY MUSHROOM RISOTTO (GLUTEN-FREE) 73

NOSTALGIC RAW-BUCKWHEAT PORRIDGE 74

MIGHTY BLACK EYED PEAS AND HAM 76
KING SIZED ALMOND RISOTTO 77
CRAZY TRUFFLE OIL RISOTTO (GLUTEN-FREE) 78
PINNACLE BANANA AND STEEL CUT OATMEAL. 80
PERFECT SPICED BLACK BEANS 82
DASHING SPINACH LENTILS STEW 83

VEGETABLES AND SIDE DISHES **85**
CRAZY PINTO BEANS 85
PINNACLE CUCUMBER QUINOA SALAD 86
PERFECT ARTICHOKE HEARTS 88
DASHING BRUSSELS SPROUTS 90
RELIABLE FRIJOLES BORRACHOS (MEXICAN "DRUNKEN BEANS") 91
CHARMING COCONUT & QUINOA CURRY (GLUTEN-FREE) 93
ENERGETIC PEPPER SOUP 94
FUNNY SAUCY BAKED BEANS 96
AWESOME ARTICHOKES AND SPINACH DIP 98

LUNCH **100**
NOSTALGIC DAL 100
BEST ROASTED BEEF 102
VINTAGE RISOTTO 103
LUCKY BEEF MEAT LOAF 105
HAPPY WARM CHICKEN SALAD 107
GREAT POTATOES WITH GROUND MEAT 109

FANTASTIC AROMATIC CONGEE 111

DELIGHTFUL BUTTER CHICKEN 113

SUPER LENTIL STEW 115

AWESOME LAMB WITH BLACK BEANS 117

ICONIC PASTA BOLOGNESE 118

Chicken And Beef **120**

QUICK MOUTHWATERING STEAK. 120

WONDERFUL INSTANT POT ROASTED CHICKEN 122

ELEGANT LEMON OLIVE CHICKEN 124

RICH EASY AND HEARTY BEEF STEW 125

TITANIC BEEF BOURGUIGNON 127

TASTY INSTANT POT CHICKEN DRUMSTICKS 129

YUMMY ITALIAN CHICKEN MARSALA 130

UNIQUE BEEF AND BROCCOLI 132

ULTIMATE VERY TENDER POT ROAST 134

ICONIC CHICKEN AVOCADO SOUP 136

Beef, Lamb, Turkey And Pork **138**

AWESOME SUNDAY BRUSSELS SPROUTS. 138

SUPER BEEF MUSHROOM STROGANOFF 139

DELIGHTFUL PORK TENDER IN TROPICAL SAUCE 141

FANTASTIC MOUTHWATERING GARLIC MEATBALLS 143

GREAT GARLIC SPICY SAUSAGE MEAL 144

MIGHTY COLLARD WITH BACON. 146

PINNACLE HOMEMADE SPAGHETTI SQUASH AND MEAT SAUCE.....147

DASHING EASTERN LAMB STEW..149

CHARMING TASTY SAUSAGE SOUP 151

PERFECT CORNED BEEF 152

PINNACLE SAVORY INSTANT SALSA PORK 154

CRAZY ITALIAN LAMB SHANKS. 156

KING SIZED KOREAN BEEF 158

MIGHTY GARLIC BEEF SIRLOIN 159

NOSTALGIC PINEAPPLE PORK 160

MEATLESS CUISINES, KETOGENIC, MAIN DISH................................162

TASTY BERRY SAUCE IN MINUTES 162

YUMMY CORNED BEEF 164

UNIQUE MUSTARD SPINACH INSTANT MEAL 165

ULTIMATE BRAISED GREEN AND RED CABBAGE 167

ICONIC BEEF BOURGUIGNON 170

AWESOME SWEET POTATO CAULIFLOWER 171

SUPER SPINACH AND EDAMAME STEW 174

DELIGHTFUL CAULIFLOWER SOUP..175

FANTASTIC QUINOA MIXED VEGETABLE 177

GREAT ZUCCHINI NOODLES IN TOMATO SOUP 178

HAPPY CHICKEN AND DELICIOUS SAUCE 181

LUCKY BROCCOLI CHICKPEA 183

VINTAGE CHICKEN MACARONI SALAD – LIMIT THIS DISH TO ONCE A WEEK 184

BEST GREEN OLIVES INSTANT POTATOES 186

NOSTALGIC DIFFERENT LASAGNA 188

MIGHTY WALNUT BEET LUNCH BOWL 190

Chapter 1: Introduction

We all dream about living a healthy lifestyle that brings us wholesome nutrition & comfort of eating healthy, tasty foods at home. We work hard to achieve success in our professional life with the aim of making our life more comforting & enjoyable. Well, Instant Pot is designed exclusively for homemakers that wished to make their kitchen time comforting & something to experience again & again.

If you're wondering over the thought of what exactly is this new Instant Pot thing, then the short & simple answer is that it is a modern kitchen revolution for current cooking needs. You can visualize an Instant Pot as a smarter version of your traditional stovetop pressure cooker. Instant Pot is a smart appliance with a feature of automation cooking that requires no constant monitoring of the food. Now all you need to do is to add food to it, set specified settings & forget about the recipe; now your Instant Pot will do all the work to bring you tasty, wholesome meals every day.

It comes with pressure setting, built-in heating element, & different cooking modules have entirely made cooking as simply as you can imagine. Instant Pot promotes automated & fast food. The structure of an Instant Pot comes with an automatic electric heating source & timer to control preset cooking time. The built-in kitchen setting off an Instant Pot lets you cook almost anything. This revolutionary appliance is not only for cooking main courses for dinner & lunch as you can prepare nutritious breakfasts in no time, satisfy your hungry stomach with go-to snacks or treat your sweet tooth with mouth-watering desserts.

You can prepare stew, soup, chili, beans, different types of meat, lentils, legumes, porridge & so much with a versatile Instant Pot. You can use it as a regular cooking appliance for sautéing, simmering or/and for simple preheating. An Instant Pot is a multipurpose kitchen revolution that works as a slow cooker, steamer, rice cooker, & yogurt maker.

In this unique Instant Pot cookbook, you'll find an exclusive collection of 100 Instant Pot recipes to prepare diverse cuisines at the comfort of your home. Now you can make hand-picked recipes from your favorite ingredients including breakfasts, appetizers, sides, grains, rice, soups, stews, main course, snacks, stocks, sauces, desserts, & yogurts as well as main course meals. This book provides exclusive sections of vegetarian meals, main course meals prepared from poultry, red meat, & seafood ingredients.

Do not wait; let is get started with making some of your favorite recipes & explore a revolutionary way of preparing cuisines.

Chapter 2: The Amazing World Of Instant Pot

Instant Pot is a good investment & quite a helpful kitchen appliance. You may also cook food, in batches, freeze them & then only heat it up later.

Cooking your favorite cuisines have never been easier. You may easily need to place all the ingredients into the pot, & your job is done. It makes use of pressured steam to help you cook tasty meals in real quick time. Instant Pot assists in sealing most of the nutrients in the food.

BEYOND THE BASIC: WHY IT IS BEING CALLED A KITCHEN REVOLUTION

Saves Time & Energy

Instant Pot takes less time to prepare food as compared to other cooking process. This appliance works especially well with dried ingredients including beans, grains, legumes, & pulses. Instead of pre-soaking them for 2 to 12 hours before cooking time, you can directly add them to the pot, along with the recommended amount of liquids and other ingredients. At high pressure, you can cook them in less than 30 to 35 minutes.

Kills Micro-Organism

In Instant Pot, the water level is heated to a high temperature where most of the unwanted micro-organisms are killed off. It kills harmful bacteria and fungus from grains & vegetables to serve you with healthy meals every time.

Nutrition Health

Unlike many other cooking process, which require you to fully immerse the vegetables & other ingredients under the water to cook them, instant pot needs just enough water to maintain high pressure the steam levels. This method prevents essential components from being washed away.

Cooking Convenience

An Instant Pot has 12-key functions which include poultry, soup, rice, beans/chili, meat/ stew, porridges, multi-grain, steam, & other control keys. Each mode has specifications for pressure & time, which can be adjusted as per your convenience.

Chapter 3: Instant Pot Buttons

Instant pot provides you with the most modern cooking functions & can cook anything for you with many pre-set cooking modules. Following are common settings for a convenient cooking experience.

- **Sauté Button:** This setting is for sautéing ingredient with the lid open; this function is for browning, sautéing or simmering of added ingredients usually oil, garlic, onions, etc.
- **Slow Cook Button:** With this function your Instant pot works as a rice cooker, which can cook to up to 40 hours, but the default setting is for 4 hours.
- **Soup Button:** With this setting you can easily prepare a wide range of broths & soups. The default is set for 30 to 35 minutes of high pressure.
- **Poultry Button:** With this setting you can easily prepare meals with poultry & the default is set at high pressure for 18 to 20 minutes.
- **Porridge Button:** With this setting you can easily prepare oatmeal or porridge of various grains. This default option makes high pressure for 20 to 25 minutes.
- **Manual Button:** With this setting, you can manually set your own pressure & cook time.

- **Bean/Chili Button:** With this setting you can easily prepare chili or beans. The default is high pressure for 30 to 35 minutes.
- **Meat/Stew Button:** With this setting you can easily prepare meats or stew & the default is set at high pressure for 35 to 40 minutes.
- **Keep Warm/Cancel Button:** With this function you can cancel any program that has been previously; it puts the cooker in standby & keeps it warm for some time.
- **Rice Button:** With this function, your Instant pot works as a rice cooker. With this setting, you can easily prepare various rice-based meals & other cuisines. The default option for this setting is automatic & cooks rice at low pressure. You can use "Adjust" setting to set your choice of time.
- **Cake & Egg Button:** This setting is to cook a wide range of cake & egg-based recipes.
- **Multigrain Button:** With this setting you can easily prepare a mixture of grains such as beans, brown rice, wild rice etc. The default option for this setting is 40 to 45 minutes of high pressure.
- **Steam Button:** You can use this function for steaming seafood, veggies or reheating foods. The default is 10 to 15 minutes of high-pressure cooking.

Yogurt Button: The default of this setting is 8 hours of cooking time to make various types of yogurts. You can also use "Adjust" to increase or decrease time.

Chapter 4: How It Works?

The Instant Pot is unlike your ordinary pressure cooker as it comes with a lot of settings thus allowing you to cook different types of foods. So how does this digital pressure cooker works? To understand how it works, it is also very crucial to know about the features & its many buttons so that it can shed light on how to use it.

Features

The Instant Pot is a nifty device that allows you to cook a myriad of dishes using one device. Below are the features of the Instant Pot that make one of the best digital pressure cookers in the market ever.

- **Many programmable settings**: You can cook certain types of foods depending on the setting that you press on the Instant Pot thus you can customize the cooking time as well as condition inside the Instant Pot. The programmable settings will be discussed later in this section.

- **Sleek exterior**: The sleek exterior of the Instant Pot doesn't only make it very simply to clean but it also adds finesse to the entire kitchen gadget.

- **Delay cooking timer**: You can transform the Instant Pot into a delayed cooker so that you can cook food at a later time so that It can be ready by the time you get back. This allows you to enjoy warm & comforting meals once you get back home.

- **Safety mechanisms**: People are afraid to use the pressure cooker because they are not so convinced about the safety features of the device. Instant Pot, on the other hand, features many safety mechanisms so that the device will function properly & not blow off if it has too much pressure. It has a pressure sensor that detects if there is too much pressure inside the pot & automatically releases it. It also has a thermostat inside so that you can monitor the exact temperature that your food is cooking. Lastly, the quick pressure release allows you to ease the pressure in the pot immediately.

- **Comes with other crucial accessories**: The Instant Pot comes with great accessories so that you can increase its functionality. The nifty accessories that come with your Instant Pot include silicone mitts, steamer rack, condensation collector, rice paddle, soup spoon, & measuring cup.

Chapter 5 - Cleaning Tips

It is crucial to clean the Instant Pot to maintain its performance. Cleaning the Instant Pot is very simply. In fact, there are so many amazing cleaning tips for the Instant Pot out there that we only included top cleaning tips to keep your digital pressure cooker spic & span.

- **Gently** separate the interior pot from the Instant Pot: Unlike other pressure cookers, the inner pot of the Instant Pot is the only thing that gets dirty. Quickly separate the interior pot for deep cleaning later. For the exterior body, please use a clean cloth moistened lightly with warm water to remove any hardened food particles. Also, never immerse the exterior body in water because it contains all the electronic components that run the all machine.

- **Now quickly** unplug from the power supply: Now before cleaning the Instant pot, please make sure that you unplug Instant Pot from the power supply so that you do not get electrocuted. This is also the time to check the cord for any damages.

- **Also** allow drying before reassembling: Allow all the parts of the Instant Pot to dry at the room temperature before reassembling everything. When reassembling, please make sure that everything is secured in place especially the electrical cords.

- Wash the interior pot with kitchen detergent: The interior pot, along with the lid, are the only washable components of the Instant Pot. Next, quickly wash them with warm soapy water. You can also place the inner pot in a dishwasher. Please make sure that you allow them to dry before assembling back to the Instant Pot.

- **Please** take care of cleaning the lid: The lid should be handled carefully as it is made up of different components. First, you need to remove the steam release handle & then check for any food particles that have been stuck. It is also really crucial to remove the silicone sealing ring & inspect for damages and hardened food particles.

Chapter 6: Instant Pot Pressure Cooking Time Charts

Your pressure cooker may have its own cooking times & temperature, always follow the instructions that came with your appliance.

The following charts provide approximate times for a wide range of foods. Because cookers & stoves vary, actual cooking times may be different.

To begin, you may want to cook for a minute or two less than the times listed.

Most times are expressed as a range because natural ingredients can vary in cooking time depending on whether they are frozen, chilled, or room temperature, how large or small the pieces are, & other factors.

When in doubt, start with the suggested time at the lower end of the range, test for doneness, & then cook your food for a few minutes if needed.

COOKING CHARTS

	Cooking Time High Pressure (minutes)	Liquid Needed	Release Method		Cooking Time High Pressure (minutes)	Liquid Needed	Release Method
Poultry							
Chicken Bones for stock	40	6 cups	NATURAL	Chicken Thigh (boneless)	4	1 cup	QUICK
Chicken Breast (bone in)	6	1 cup	QUICK	Chicken, Whole	20	1 ½ cups	NATURAL
Chicken Breast (boneless)	4	1 cup	QUICK	Cornish Game Hen (1 to ½)	8	1 cup	NATURAL
Chicken Thigh (bone in)	7	1 cup	QUICK	Turkey Breast (boneless 2 to 3 pounds)	20 to 25	1 ½ cup	NATURAL
Beef							
Beef Bones for stock	40	6 cups	NATURAL	Meatloaf	35	1 ½ cups	NATURAL
Brisket (3 ½ to 4 pounds)	55 to 65	1 ½ cups	NATURAL	Pot Roast (3 ½ to 4 pounds)	55 to 65	2 cups	NATURAL
Corned Beef Brisket	55	covered	NATURAL	Short Ribs	55	1 ½ cups	NATURAL
Flank Steak (1 pound)	25	1 cup	NATURAL	Stew Meat (1-inch cubes)	15 to 20	1 cup	NATURAL
Ground Beef	5	1 cup	QUICK	Veal Shanks	20 to 25	1 ½ cups	NATURAL
Meatballs	5	1 cup	NATURAL	Veal Stew Meat (1-inch cubes)	20 to 25	1 ½ cups	NATURAL

ELECTRIC PRESSURE COOKING DIRECTIONS
RICE, GRAIN AND BEANS

	Amount	Cooking Time	Temperature
White, long grain rice	1 cup rice-1 ½ cup water	6 minutes	High
White, short grain rice	1 cup rice-1 ½ cup water	6 minutes	High
Brown, long grain rice	1 cup rice-1 ½ cup water	12 minutes	High
Brown short grain rice	1 cup rice-1 ¾ cup water	12 minutes	High
Quinoa	1 cup quinoa-2 cups water	6 minutes	High
Kamut	1 cup kamut-2 cups water	30 minutes	High
Couscous	1 cup cuscous-2 cups water	3 minutes	High
Amaranth	1 cup grain-3 cups water	4 minutes	High
Millet	1 cup grain-2 cups water	6 minutes	High
Spelt	1 cup grain-3 cups water	30 minutes	High
Steel cut oats	1 cup oats-2 cups water	4 minutes	High
Wheat berries	1 cup wheat-3 cups water	30 minutes	High
Barley, pearl	1 cup barley-4 cups water	20 minutes	High
Bulgur	1 cup bulgur-3 cups water	10 minutes	High
Pinto Beans	1 cup beans-3 cups water	50 minutes	High
Black Beans	1 cup beans-3 cups water	50 minutes	High
Great Northern/Red Beans	1 cup beans-3 cups water	50 minutes	High
Kidney Beans/Red Beans	1 cup beans-3 cups water	50 minutes	High
Lentils	1 cup beans-3 cups water	30 minutes	High
Black-Eyed Peas	1 cup beans-3 cups water	30 minutes	High
Chick Peas/Garbanzo	1 cup beans-3 cups water	30 minutes	High
Cannellini Beans/White Kidney	1 cup beans-3 cups water	30 minutes	High
Lima Beans	1 cup beans-3 cups water	25 minutes	High

Pork

Baby Back Ribs	30	1 cup	NATURAL	Pork Chops (boneless, 1-inch)	4 to 5	1 ½ cups	NATURAL
Country Style Ribs	20 to 25	1 ½ cups	NATURAL	Pork Loin (2 to 2 ½ pounds)	25	1 ½ cups	NATURAL
Ground Pork	5	1 cup	QUICK	Pork Shoulder (3 pounds)	55	1 ½ cups	NATURAL
Ham (bone in, 5 pounds, pre cooked)	25 to 30	1 ½ cups	NATURAL	Sausages	10 to 15	1 ½ cups	QUICK
Meatballs	5	1 cup	NATURAL	Spare Ribs	45	1 cup	NATURAL
Pork Chops (bone in, 1-inch)	6	1 /2 cups	NATURAL	Stew Meat (1-inch cubes)	15 to 20	1 cup	NATURAL

Lamb

Ground Lamb	5	1 cup	QUICK	Leg of Lamb (boneless, 3 ½ to 4 pounds)	35 to 45	1 ½ cups	NATURAL
Lamb Shanks	30	1 ½ cups	NATURAL	Stew Meat (1-inch cubes)	15 to 20	1 cup	NATURAL
Meatballs	5	1 cup	NATURAL				

Fish and Seafood

Calamari	20	5 cups	QUICK	Mussels	4	2 cups	QUICK
Clams	4	1 cup	QUICK	Salmon	5	4 cups	QUICK
Crabs Legs	4	1 cup	QUICK	Shrimp	2	3 cups	QUICK
Fish Fillet (1-inch thick)	5	6 cups	QUICK				

Measurement Conversion Chart

The charts below will help you to convert between different units of volume in US customary units.

Please note that US volume is not the same as in the UK & other countries, & many of the measurements are different depending on which country you're in.

It is very simply to get confused when dealing with US & UK units! The only possible good thing is that the metric units never change!

All the measurement charts below are for US customary units only!

Also every effort has been made to ensure that the Measurement Charts on this page are accurate.

American and British Variances

Term	Abbreviation	Nationality	Dry or liquid	Metric equivalent	Equivalent in context
cup	c., C.		usually liquid	237 milliliters	16 tablespoons or 8 ounces
ounce	fl oz, fl. oz.	American	liquid only	29.57 milliliters	
		British	either	28.41 milliliters	
gallon	gal.	American	liquid only	3.785 liters	4 quarts
		British	either	4.546 liters	4 quarts
inch	in, in.			2.54 centimeters	
ounce	oz, oz.	American	dry	28.35 grams	1/16 pound
			liquid	see OUNCE	see OUNCE
pint	p., pt.	American	liquid	0.473 liter	1/8 gallon or 16 ounces
			dry	0.551 liter	1/2 quart
		British	either	0.568 liter	
pound	lb.		dry	453.592 grams	16 ounces
Quart	q., qt, qt.	American	liquid	0.946 liter	1/4 gallon or 32 ounces
			dry	1.101 liters	2 pints
		British	either	1.136 liters	
Teaspoon	t., tsp., tsp		either	about 5 milliliters	1/3 tablespoon
Tablespoon	T., tbs., tbsp.		either	about 15 milliliters	3 teaspoons or 1/2 ounce

Volume (Liquid)

American Standard (Cups & Quarts)	American Standard (Ounces)	Metric (Milliliters & Liters)
2 tbsp.	1 fl. oz.	30 ml
1/4 cup	2 fl. oz.	60 ml
1/2 cup	4 fl. oz.	125 ml
1 cup	8 fl. oz.	250 ml
1 1/2 cups	12 fl. oz.	375 ml
2 cups or 1 pint	16 fl. oz.	500 ml
4 cups or 1 quart	32 fl. oz.	1000 ml or 1 liter
1 gallon	128 fl. oz.	4 liters

Oven Temperatures

American Standard	Metric
250° F	130° C
300° F	150° C
350° F	180° C
400° F	200° C
450° F	230° C

Weight (Mass)

American Standard (Ounces)	Metric (Grams)
1/2 ounce	15 grams
1 ounce	30 grams
3 ounces	85 grams
3.75 ounces	100 grams
4 ounces	115 grams
8 ounces	225 grams
12 ounces	340 grams
16 ounces or 1 pound	450 grams

Volume (Dry)

American Standard	Metric
1/8 teaspoon	5 ml
1/4 teaspoon	1 ml
1/2 teaspoon	2 ml
3/4 teaspoon	4 ml
1 teaspoon	5 ml
1 tablespoon	15 ml
1/4 cup	59 ml
1/3 cup	79 ml
1/2 cup	118 ml
2/3 cup	158 ml
3/4 cup	177 ml
1 cup	225 ml
2 cups or 1 pint	450 ml
3 cups	675 ml
4 cups or 1 quart	1 liter
1/2 gallon	2 liters
1 gallon	4 liters

Chapter 7: Recipes

NOW GO AHEAD AND CHECK OUT THESE AMAZING RECIPES.

Breakfast

Yummy Breakfast Espresso Oatmeal

Who wants to try this one?

Ingredients:

- 1 cup milk
- About 2.5 tablespoons grated chocolate
- 1 cup oats
- 2 tablespoons sugar
- About 1.5 teaspoon espresso powder
- A dollop of whipped cream
- 1/4 teaspoon salt
- 2 1/2 cups water
- 2 teaspoons vanilla extract

Directions:

1. First of all, please make sure you've all the ingredients available. Place all ingredients except for the whipped cream & chocolate shavings in the Instant Pot.
2. Then stir to combine everything.
3. Lock the lid & close the vent.
4. Press High Pressure and set the cooking time to about 10 to 15 minutes.

5. One thing remains to be done. Now once done, do quick pressure release
6. Finally serve with whip cream & sprinkle with chocolate shavings on top.

Serves: 4 to 5

Preparation Time: 5 to 10 minutes

Cooking Time: 10 to 15 minutes

The next big recipe…

Nutritional information:

Calories per serving: 173

Carbohydrates: 35.5g

Protein: 6.4g

Fat: 5.1g

Fiber: 4g

Unique Coconut Cornmeal Porridge

Certainly a show stopper.

Ingredients:

- 1 1/4 cups coconut milk
- 3/4 cup sweetened condensed milk
- 1 1/4 cups yellow cornmeal, fine

- About 1 teaspoon coconut flakes
- 2 1/2 sticks cinnamon
- 1 1/4 teaspoons vanilla extract
- 6 cups water

Directions:

1. First of all, please make sure you've all the ingredients available. Add 5 cups of water & all the coconut milk to the Instant Pot.
2. Now mix the cornmeal with 1 cup of water & add the mixture to the pot.
3. This step is important. Stir in vanilla extract, coconut flakes, & cinnamon sticks.
4. Then secure the lid of the cooker & press the "Manual" function key.
5. Adjust the time to about 5 to 10 minutes and cook properly at high pressure.
6. One thing remains to be done. After the beep, release the pressure naturally & remove the lid.
7. Finally stir in sweetened condensed milk.

Serves: 6 to 7

Prep Time: 15 to 20 minutes

Cooking Time: 5 to 10 minutes

I use to have it during my exams.

Nutritional information:

Calories: 253

Carbohydrate: 46.2g

Protein: 6.9g

Fat: 3.1g

Sugar: 17.2g

Sodium: 179mg

Ultimate Delicious Vanilla Steel Cut Oats

You can make this very easily.

Ingredients:

- 1 cup steel cut oats
- Grated chocolate for serving
- 2 and 1/2 cups water
- Whipped cream for serving
- About 2.5 tablespoons sugar
- A pinch of salt
- 2 teaspoons vanilla extract
- 1 teaspoon espresso powder
- 1 cup milk

Directions:

1. First of all, please make sure you've all the ingredients available. Now in your instant pot, mix oats with milk, water, sugar, salt and espresso powder, stir, cover and cook properly on High for about 10 to 15 minutes. Cover the pot & cook at High for 10 minutes.
2. Finally add vanilla extract, stir, leave everything aside for about 5 to 10 minutes, divide into bowls & serve with whipped cream and grated chocolate on top. Enjoy!

Preparation time: 10 to 15 minutes

Cooking time: 10 to 15 minutes

Servings: 4 to 5

Ready, set, go….

Nutritional information:

Calories 250

Fat 3.1

Fiber 5.4

Carbs 43

Sugar 4

Protein 5

Iconic Scotch Eggs With Ground Sausage
A little different, a little extra ordinary.

Ingredients:

- 1 lb. of ground sausage
- 1/2 Teaspoon of dried mint
- About 1.5 Tbsp. of vegetable oil
- 1 pinch of black pepper
- 1 Pinch of salt
- 4 Eggs

Directions:

1. First of all, please make sure you've all the ingredients available. Place the steaming basket in your Instant Pot. Then pour 1 cup of water with the eggs.
2. Now close the lid of your Instant Pot and set it at high pressure for around 5 to 10 minutes.
3. When the timer beeps, naturally release the pressure for around for about 5 to 10 minutes, then apply a quick release & turn off the Instant Pot.
4. This step is important. Cool the eggs into cold water; then remove its shells & split the sausage into pieces of equal size.
5. Then season the sausage with the salt, the pepper & the mint and combine it very well with your fingers.
6. Flatten the sausage meat into equal pieces & place your hard boiled eggs right into the centre & then wrap your sausage around it.
7. Now repeat it with the rest of the egg halves.
8. Press the button sauté or browning in your Instant Put & add a little bit if oil (No more than 3 tbsp.) and sauté your scotch eggs.

9. Then once done with sautéing, remove the eggs from the Instant Pot & pour 1 cup of water into it.
10. One thing remains to be done. Place the trivet & line the eggs above the rack or the trivet.
11. Finally set at high pressure for around 5 to 10 minutes and when the timer beeps, quick release the pressure & serve your scotch rolls. Enjoy!

Time: 15 to 20 minutes

Servings: 4 to 6

Legend overload...

Nutritional information:

Calories 280g

Fats 18.7g

Cholesterol 0mg

Total Carbohydrates 16g

Protein 12g

Awesome Ham & Egg Casserole

Most fantastic recipe ever.

Ingredients:

- 1 cup ham (Diced)
- About 1 teaspoon black pepper
- 1/4 cup chives (Chopped)
- 1/2 cup plain Greek yogurt
- 6 eggs
- 1 cup cheddar cheese (Shredded)

Directions:

1. First of all, please make sure you've all the ingredients available. In a bowl of medium size, thoroughly whisk the eggs & yogurt.
2. Then stir in the cheese, chives, ham, and pepper.
3. Place your Instant Pot on a flat kitchen surface; plug it & turn it on.
4. This step is important. Open the lid, & one by one add the mixture into the pot. Carefully close its lid and firmly lock it.
5. Now after, seal the valve too.
6. To start making the recipe, press "Slow Cook" button.
7. You have to set cooking time; set the timer for about 85 to 90 minutes.
8. Now allow the pot to cook the mixture until the timer goes off.
9. One thing remains to be done. Turn off the pot & press "Cancel." Let the built up pressure to vent out naturally; it will take 5 to 10 minutes to completely release inside pressure.
10. Finally open its lid. Make wedges & serve warm!

Prep Time: 25 to 30 min.

Cooking Time: 1 hour 25 to 30 min.

Number of Servings: 2 to 3

Nostalgic feeling...

Nutritional information:

Calories - 639

Fat – 42.8g

Carbohydrates – 9.5g

Fiber – 1.9g

Protein – 50.4g

Super Oatmeal With Nuts

Jumpstart your taste. ?

Ingredients:

- 4 tablespoons almond flakes
- About 1 teaspoon cardamom
- 1/4 cup pecans
- 2 cups oatmeal
- 1 teaspoon vanilla extract

- 1 cup water
- About 3.5 tablespoons brown sugar
- 2 cups milk
- 1 cup cream
- 1/4 cup walnuts

Directions:

1. First of all, please make sure you've all the ingredients available. Crush the walnuts and pecans & combine them together.
2. Now Put the oatmeal, water, brown sugar, milk, cream, vanilla extract, and cardamom in the Instant Pot.
3. Set the Instant Pot mode to "Porridge," & cook properly for about 5 to 10 minutes.
4. One thing remains to be done. Then remove the oatmeal from the Instant Pot & stir.
5. Finally sprinkle the dish with the almond flakes & serve.

Prep time: 5 to 10 minutes

Cooking time: 2 to 5 minutes

Servings: 6 to 8

Simplicity is best.

Nutritional information:

Calories 260

Fat 16.7

Fiber 2

carbs 22.71

protein 6

Delightful Creamy Banana Breakfast Bread

Oh yeah. This is the recipe I was waiting for.

Ingredients:

- 3 ripe bananas (Chopped)
- Maple syrup (optional)
- 1/4 cup Philadelphia cheese
- 1/4 cup walnuts (Chopped)
- 3 eggs
- 1/2 cup 2.5% milk
- About 2.5 tbsp coconut oil, melted
- 2 tbsp sugar
- 6 slices of toast bread, cubed
- About 1 tsp ground cinnamon

Directions:

1. First of all, please make sure you've all the ingredients available. Cut the toast bread into cubes.
2. Now grease baking dish with a bit of coconut oil & place 1 layer of bread cubes.
3. This step is important. Cover the bread layer with a layer of 1 chopped banana & cover them with Philadelphia cheese.

4. Repeat the steps, creating as many layers as you want.
5. Then sprinkle the layers with chopped walnuts.
6. In a medium or large bowl, please whisk the eggs with sugar, cinnamon, milk, and vanilla, & carefully pour the mixture over the layers.
7. Now put 1 cup of water into your instant pot and install the steaming rack. Place the baking dish on the trivet.
8. One thing remains to be done. Secure the lid, select "Porridge" & set the timer for about 30 to 35 minutes.
9. Finally when the time is up, quick-release the pressure, remove the lid & serve with maple syrup.

Preparation time: 15 to 20 min

Cooking time: 30 to 35 min

Servings: 6 to 7

Legendary taste.

Nutritional information:

Calories: 61

Protein: 6g

Fats: 20g

Carbs: 45g

Fantastic Cheese Quiche

Light taste.

Ingredients:

- 1/2 Cup of milk
- 1 Cup of shredded cheese
- About 1/2 Teaspoon of salt
- 2 Large chopped green onions
- 1/8 Teaspoon of ground black pepper
- 4 Slices of bacon and crumbled cooked
- 1/2 Cup of diced ham
- 1 Cup of cooked ground sausage
- 6 large and well beaten eggs

Directions:

1. First of all, please make sure you've all the ingredients available. Start by putting the trivet into the bottom of your Instant Pot; then add 1 & 1/2 cups of water to it.
2. Now at the same time and in a separate bowl, place the eggs, the milk, the salt & the pepper; then mix all of the ingredients together and whisk.
3. This step is important. Add the bacon, the sausage, the ham, the green onions & the cheese until around 1 quart of your soufflé dish is covered.
4. Then pour the mixture of the eggs over the top of your meat & stir very well.
5. Cover your soufflé dish and use an aluminium foil to place your pan on the trivet in the Instant Pot.
6. Now close the lid and set high pressure for around 30 to 35 minutes.

7. One thing remains to be done. When the timer beeps, turn off your Instant Pot & quick release the pressure.
8. Finally sprinkle cheese & broil the quiche until it becomes golden; then serve and enjoy!

Time: 30 to 35 minutes

Servings: 3 to 4

As the name suggests….

Nutritional information:

Calories 139g

Fats 5g

Cholesterol 40.0mg

Total Carbohydrates 14g

Protein 9g

Great Fruited Steel-Cut Breakfast Oats

Magical…

Ingredients:

- 1/2 cup plain Greek yogurt
- About 2.5 tablespoons slivered almonds
- 1 1/2 cup water
- 2 apples, cored and chopped

- 1/2 teaspoon cinnamon powder
- 1/4 cup maple syrup
- 1 cup steel cut oats
- About 1 teaspoon cloves

Directions:

1. First of all, please make sure you've all the ingredients available. Place the oats in the Instant Pot.
2. Now stir in the water, yogurt, cloves, apples, maple syrup, and cinnamon.
3. Close the lid and seal the valve.
4. Then press the Manual button & cook properly for about 2 to 5 minutes.
5. One thing remains to be done. Do quick pressure release.
6. Finally stir again and garnish with slivered almonds & more maple syrup or cinnamon.

Serves: 2 to 4

Preparation Time: 2 to 5 minutes

Cooking Time: 5 to 10 minutes

Right on track.

Nutritional information:

Calories per serving:330

Carbohydrates: 83.9g

Protein: 10.4g

Fat: 4.3g

Fiber: 12.1g

Happy Strawberry Cream Oatmeal

Believe me...

Ingredients:

- 2 1/4 cups water
- 8 strawberries (Chopped)
- 2 1/4 cups milk
- 1/4 cup sugar
- About 1 teaspoon salt
- 2 cups old-fashioned oats
- 1/2 teaspoon ground cinnamon

Directions:

1. First of all, please make sure you've all the ingredients available. Next, quickly add all the ingredients to the Instant Pot. Save a few strawberry slices for garnishing.
2. Now secure the lid of the cooker & press the "Multigrain option."
3. Adjust the time to about 5 to 10 minutes and let it cook.
4. One thing remains to be done. After the beep, release the pressure naturally & remove the lid.
5. Finally serve with the chopped strawberries on top.

Serves: 4 to 6

Prep time: 5 to 10 minutes

Cooking time: 5 to 10 minutes

Always kept wondering how it was made... One day I sat beside my chef and got it.

Nutritional information:

Calories: 436

Carbohydrate: 75g

Protein: 14.7g

Fat: 8g

Sugar: 22g

Sodium: 360mg

Fish And Seafood

Fantastic Creamy Coconut Fish Curry

Best combo ever... Don't you agree?

Ingredients:

- 2 cups coconut milk
- Salt
- About 3.5 tbsp curry powder

- 1/2 tsp ground fenugreek
- 1 tomato (Chopped)
- 1 tsp chili powder
- 1/2 tsp ground turmeric
- 2 green chilies (Sliced)
- About 2.5 tsp ground cumin
- 1 tbsp ground coriander
- 2 medium onions (Sliced)
- 6 bay leaves
- About 1.5 tbsp fresh ginger, grated
- 2 garlic cloves
- 1 1/2 lbs fish fillets, rinsed and cut into pieces

Directions:

1. First of all, please make sure you've all the ingredients available. Spray instant pot from inside with cooking spray. Set the instant pot on sauté mode.
2. Then add garlic, ginger, and onion to the pot and sauté for about 2 minutes.
3. This step is important. Add all ground spices and sauté for about 2 to 5 minutes.
4. Add coconut milk and stir well.
5. Now add tomatoes, fish, & green chilies. Stir well.
6. Please gently seal the pot with lid & cook on manual high pressure for about 5 to 10 minutes.
7. Release pressure using quick release method than open the lid.
8. One thing remains to be done. Season with salt.
9. Finally stir well & serve.

Serves: 4 to 5

Preparation time: 10 to 15 minutes

Cooking time: 15 to 20 minutes

Someone is definitely ready for this.

Nutritional information:

Calories: 726

Total Fat: 50.8g

Saturated Fat: 30.4g

Protein: 29.7g

Carbs: 46.8g

Fiber: 7.1g

Sugar: 7g

Great Butter Shrimp Paella

Good recipe!!

Ingredients:

- 1/4 cup parsley (Chopped)

- Cilantro to sprinkle
- About 1.5 teaspoon salt
- 2 cups chicken broth
- 1 lemon, juiced
- 1 teaspoon saffron
- 4 cloves garlic (Chopped)
- 1 pound shrimps
- About 1.5 pound fish fillet
- Red pepper as needed
- 1 cup long grain rice
- Pepper as needed
- 1/4 cup butter

Directions:

1. First of all, please make sure you've all the ingredients available. Place your Instant Pot on a flat kitchen surface; plug it & turn it on.
2. Now open the lid, and one by one add the shrimps, water, and fish in the pot.
3. Carefully close its lid and firmly lock it. Then after, seal the valve too.
4. This step is important. To start making the recipe, press "Manual" button.
5. You have to set cooking time; set the timer for about 5 to 10 minutes.
6. Then allow the pot to cook the mixture until the timer goes off.
7. Turn off the pot & press "Cancel."

8. Allow the built up pressure to vent out naturally; it will take 5 to 10 minutes to completely release inside pressure.
9. Now open its lid and add the butter, pepper, rice, and salt and mix.
10. Add the red pepper, garlic & lemon juice; combine well.
11. Add the saffron to the broth. Close the lid; press "Manual" button.
12. Then you have to set cooking time; set the timer for about 20 to 25 minutes.
13. One thing remains to be done. Allow the pot to cook the mixture properly until the timer goes off. Quick release pressure.
14. Finally sprinkle cilantro on top & serve warm!

Prep Time: 5 to 10 min.

Cooking Time: 25 to 30 min.

Number of Servings: 8 to 10

Lucky!!

Nutritional information:

Calories - 397

Fat – 23g

Carbohydrates – 25.4g

Fiber – 2g

Protein – 19g

Happy Calamari In Tomato Sauce

Yes, this is famous!!

Ingredients:

- 1 white onion
- 1 teaspoon lime juice
- About 1.5 teaspoon cilantro
- 3 garlic cloves
- 1/2 teaspoon ground white pepper
- 1 teaspoon ground ginger
- 1/4 cup fish stock
- About 1.5 teaspoon fresh thyme
- 3 medium tomatoes
- 1/4 cup wine
- 1/4 cup water
- 12 ounces calamari
- 1 tablespoon olive oil

Directions:

1. First of all, please make sure you've all the ingredients available. Wash the calamari carefully and peel it.
2. Now slice the calamari into medium-thick slices.

3. Slice the garlic cloves, dice the onion, and c. hop the fresh thyme and tomatoes.
4. This step is important. Set the Instant Pot to "Sauté" mode.
5. Then put the sliced calamari into the Instant Pot & sprinkle it with the olive oil. Sauté the dish for about 5 to 10 minutes.
6. Add the garlic, thyme, onion, & tomatoes to the Instant Pot.
7. Now sprinkle the dish with the water, ground ginger, wine, lime juice, and fish stock, stir well, and close the lid.
8. One thing remains to be done. Set the Instant Pot to "Meat/Stew" mode. Stew the dish for about 5 to 10 minutes.
9. Finally remove the cooked calamari from the Instant Pot. Serve the dish hot.

Prep time: 10 to 15 minutes

Cooking time: 15 to 20 minutes

Servings: 4 to 6

Wow, that's cute!!

Nutritional information:

Calories 238

Fat 6.1

Fiber 2

Carbs 16.64

Protein 29

Lucky Spicy Cajun & Lime Shrimp (Gluten-Free)

Fresh start with something new!!

Ingredients:

- 1 bunch fresh asparagus
- Lime wedges
- About 1 tbsp Cajun seasoning – please check the ingredients
- 1 pound fresh peeled shrimp

Directions:

1. First of all, please make sure you've all the ingredients available. Put 1 cup of still water to the Instant Pot.
2. Now insert the steam rack & place asparagus on it.
3. Carefully put the shrimp on the asparagus & season with Cajun to taste.
4. One thing remains to be done. Then secure the lid, select "Steam" & cook properly at low pressure for about 2 minutes.
5. Finally when the time is up, quick-release the pressure & serve immediately and lime wedges.

Preparation time: 5 to 10 min

Cooking time: 5 to 10 min

Servings: 4 to 6

Try this my way!!

Nutritional information:

Calories: 126

Protein: 4.6 g

Fats: 18g

Carbs: 2.2g

Vintage Mussels In Citrus Juice And Dry White Wine

I don't know about you, but I include this one everytime I get a chance.

Ingredients:

- 2 dozen mussels, cleaned
- Pinch of pepper, to taste
- 1 cup cornmeal
- About 2.5 garlic cloves (Minced)
- 1 tbsp. lemon juice, freshly squeezed
- Pinch of salt
- 1 tbsp. orange juice, freshly squeezed
- 5 cups cold water
- About 2.5 tbsp. parsley (Minced)
- 2/3 cup dry white wine
- 1/2 cup Italian prosciutto (Chopped)

- 1/2 cup olive oil
- About 2.5 tbsp. cilantro, minced

Directions:

1. First of all, please make sure you've all the ingredients available. Put together cornmeal & mussels in a mixing bowl.
2. Now pour cold water & make sure mussels are submerged.
3. Let mussels soak for 1 hour.
4. After an hour, ensure that mussels are rinsed well.
5. This step is important. Meanwhile, pour olive oil into the Instant Pot Pressure Cooker. Press the "saute" button.
6. Then sauté garlic and Italian prosciutto for about 2 to 5 minutes. Season with salt and pepper.
7. Pour orange and lemon juice, dry white wine, and mussels.
8. Lock the lid in place. Press the high pressure & cook properly for about 2 to 5 minutes.
9. Now when the beep sounds, Choose the Quick Pressure Release.
10. One thing remains to be done. This will depressurize for about 5 to 10 minutes. Remove the lid.
11. Finally garnish with cilantro & parsley on top. Serve.

Serves: 2 to 4

RECOMMENDED SERVING SIZE: 11/2 cups

Baking does the trick!!

Nutritional information:

Calories – 146

Carbohydrates – 0 gram

Fat – 4 grams

Protein – 20 grams

Best Fish Curry

I repeat... Try it if you want to. No regrets. Right!!

Ingredients:

- 1 tomato (Chopped)
- About 2.5 tablespoons lemon juice
- 14 ounces coconut milk
- 1 teaspoon hot pepper flakes
- 2 onions (Sliced)
- 2 capsicums, cut into strips
- About 2.5 garlic cloves (Minced)
- 1/2 teaspoon fenugreek, ground
- 6 curry leaves
- 1 tablespoons coriander, ground
- Salt and black pepper to the taste
- 1 tablespoon ginger, finely grated
- 1/2 teaspoon turmeric, ground
- 2 teaspoons cumin, ground

- 6 fish fillets, cut into medium pieces

Directions:

1. First of all, please make sure you've all the ingredients available. Set your instant pot on Sauté mode, add oil & curry leaves and fry for about 2 minutes.
2. Then add ginger, onion and garlic, stir and cook properly for about 2 to 5 minutes.
3. Add coriander, cumin, turmeric, fenugreek and hot pepper, stir and cook properly for about 2 to 5 minutes.
4. One thing remains to be done. Now add coconut milk, tomatoes, fish and capsicum, stir, cover and cook on Low for about 5 to 10 minutes.
5. Finally add salt and pepper to the taste, stir, divide into bowls, & serve with lemon juice on top. Enjoy!

Preparation time: 10 to 15 minutes

Cooking time: 15 to 20 minutes

Servings: 6 to 7

Why not??

Nutritional information:

Calories 230

Fat 10

Fiber 3

Carbs 12

Protein 23

Nostalgic Sweet Soy Fish

Leave a mark!!

Ingredients:

- 3 tablespoons vegetable oil
- 3 tablespoons soy sauce
- About 2.5 teaspoons minced garlic
- 3 teaspoons sliced shallot
- 2 teaspoons chopped red chili
- 1-inch galangal
- 1 lb. fresh trout
- About 1.5 bay leaf

Directions:

1. First of all, please make sure you've all the ingredients available. Preheat an Instant Pot for about 30 to 35 seconds then select the "Sauté" menu.
2. Now pour vegetable oil into the Instant Pot then brown the trout.

3. Take the browned trout out from the Instant Pot then set aside.
4. This step is important. Discard the oil then return the browned trout into the Instant Pot.
5. Then sprinkle minced garlic, sliced shallot, & red chili over the trout then add galangal and bay leaf.
6. Drizzle soy sauce over the trout then cover the Instant Pot properly.
7. Now select "Manual" setting then cook the spaghetti properly on high for about 5 to 10 minutes.
8. One thing remains to be done. Once it is done, quickly release the Instant Pot then open the lid.
9. Finally transfer to a serving dish then enjoy immediately.

Serves: 2 to 4

Preparation time: 5 to 10 minutes

Cooking time: 10 to 15 minutes

Spice up!!

Nutritional information:

Calories: 258

Total Fat: 22g

Saturated Fat: 4.3g

Protein: 10.7g

Carbs: 5g

Fiber: 0.6g

Sugar: 0.9g

Mighty Spicy Chili Snapper

What do you think? ?

Ingredients:

- 1 red snapper, cleaned
- A pinch of sea salt
- About 3.5 tablespoons chili paste
- 1 teaspoon sesame oil
- 1 tablespoon soy sauce
- 1 green onion (Chopped)
- 2 cups water
- About 2.5 teaspoons sesame seeds, toasted
- 1 garlic clove (Minced)
- 2 teaspoons sugar
- 1/2 teaspoon ginger, grated

Directions:

1. First of all, please make sure you've all the ingredients available. Make some slits into the snapper and season with some salt and leave aside for about 25 to 30 minutes.
2. Now place your Instant Pot on a flat kitchen surface; plug it & turn it on.

3. Pour the water into the pot. Arrange the steamer basket in the pot & add the fish over the trivet.
4. Rub the snapper with the chili paste.
5. This step is important. Carefully close its lid and firmly lock it. Then after, seal the valve too.
6. Then to start making the recipe, press "Manual" button.
7. You have to set cooking time; set the timer for about 10 to 15 minutes.
8. Allow the pot to cook the mixture properly until the timer goes off.
9. Turn off the pot & press "Cancel."
10. Now allow the built up pressure to vent out naturally; it will take 5 to 10 minutes to completely release inside pressure.
11. Open its lid and transfer the cooked mixture into serving container/containers.
12. One thing remains to be done. In a bowl of medium size, thoroughly mix the sugar with soy sauce, sesame seeds, garlic, ginger, sesame oil and green onion.
13. Finally serve the fish with the prepared sauce!

Prep Time: 20 to 25 min.

Cooking Time: 10 to 15 min.

Number of Servings: 2 to 3

What makes this the best? Check it out for yourself!!

Nutritional information:

Calories - 186

Fat – 12g

Carbohydrates – 23.5g

Fiber – 1g

Protein – 6.2g

King Sized Marjoram Salmon

Just got better!!

Ingredients:

- 1 tablespoon marjoram
- About 1.5 teaspoon onion powder
- 1/2 teaspoon rosemary
- 1 teaspoon butter
- 1 tablespoons salt
- 1/2 cup dill
- About 1.5 tablespoon paprika
- 1 cup water
- 1 pound salmon fillet
- 1 teaspoon cilantro

Directions:

1. First of all, please make sure you've all the ingredients available. Combine the rosemary, marjoram, and salt in a small bowl.
2. Then rub the salmon fillet with the spice mixture.
3. Now quickly chop the dill & then combine it with the onion powder & paprika in a mixing bowl. Add cilantro and stir well.
4. This step is important. Place the salmon fillet on the steamer rack & transfer it to the Instant Pot. Set the Instant Pot to "Steam" mode.
5. Now sprinkle the salmon with the dill mixture.
6. Close the Instant Pot and cook the fish properly for about 15 to 20 minutes.
7. One thing remains to be done. When the cooking time ends, release the remaining pressure & let the salmon rest briefly.
8. Finally transfer the dish to a serving plate.

Prep time: 10 to 15 minutes

Cooking time: 15 to 20 minutes

Servings: 6 to 7

Got the idea!!

Nutritional information:

Calories 127

Fat 6.2

Fiber 1

Carbs 1.17

Protein 16

Crazy Salmon & Spinach Penne

Relax and enjoy this recipe!!

Ingredients:

- About 1.5 tbsp olive oil
- Pesto sauce to taste
- 4 cups still water
- Salt and pepper to taste
- 10 ounces smoked salmon, chopped into small pieces
- 1/2 cup heavy cream
- About 1.5 tsp lemon juice
- 1 cup parmesan cheese, grated
- 16 ounces dry penne

Directions:

1. First of all, please make sure you've all the ingredients available. Put the penne, 4 cups of water & 1 tbsp olive oil in the pot.
2. Now close the lid, select "Manual" & cook properly at high pressure for about 2 to 5 minutes.
3. Let the pressure release for several minutes & then quick-release the remaining pressure.
4. Then carefully remove the lid, add the pieces of smoked salmon, heavy cream, lemon juice, 1/2 cup grated

parmesan and spinach leaves & stir well with a wooden spatula.
5. One thing remains to be done. Press "Saute" & continue cooking for several minutes until the leaves wilt down.
6. Finally serve immediately with the remaining 1/2 cup grated parmesan & pesto sauce.

Preparation time: 10 to 15 min

Cooking time: 15 to 20 min

Servings: 8 to 9

Got the idea!!

Try this one if you're hungry!!

Nutritional information:

Calories: 420

Protein: 13 g

Fats: 11g

Carbs: 66g

Poultry And Chicken

Yummy Chicken Pot Pie

What do you think?

Ingredients:

- 1/3 cup celery (Sliced)
- About 1/4 tsp pepper
- 2/3 cup frozen mixed vegetables
- 1 cup chicken broth
- 1/4 tsp poultry seasoning
- About 1/2 tsp dried thyme
- 10 oz chicken thighs, boneless and skinless
- 1/4 cup onion (Chopped)

Directions:

1. First of all, please make sure you've all the ingredients available. Next, please use the "Slow Cooker" setting on your Instant Pot.
2. Now quickly add all ingredients except frozen vegetables into the slow cooker & mix well.
3. Cover and cook properly on low for about 3 to 4 hours.
4. One thing remains to be done. Then add frozen vegetables and cook properly on high for another 30 to 35 minutes.
5. Finally serve & enjoy.

Total Time: 4 hours 40 to 45 minutes

Serves: 2 to 3

Time for an iconic recipe.

Nutritional information:

Calories 338

Fat 11.3 g

Carbohydrates 10.5 g

Sugar 3.1 g

Protein 45.5 g

Cholesterol 126 mg

Tasty Classic Spiced Chicken Breasts

Magical taste.

Ingredients:

- 1/8 teaspoon oregano (Dried)
- 1 cup water
- About 1/4 teaspoon dried basil
- 3 chicken breasts, boneless and skinless
- 1 tablespoon olive oil
- 1/4 teaspoon garlic powder
- About 1/4 teaspoon black pepper
- 1/2 teaspoon salt

Directions:

1. First of all, please make sure you've all the ingredients available. In a mixing bowl of medium size, combine the garlic powder, oregano, salt, black pepper, and basil.

2. Now rinse the chicken, pat dry and season one side with the 1/2 portion of the prepared mix.
3. Place your Instant Pot on a flat kitchen surface; plug it & turn it on.
4. To start making the recipe, press "Sauté" button.
5. This step is important. Add the oil & chicken, seasoned side down and then season the second side as well using remaining seasoning mix; cook properly for about 2 to 5 minutes per side to soften the ingredients.
6. Remove from the pot. Pour the water into the pot.
7. Then arrange the trivet in the pot & add the chicken over the trivet.
8. Carefully close its lid and firmly lock it. Then after, seal the valve too.
9. To start making the recipe, press "Manual" button.
10. Then you have to set cooking time; set the timer for about 5 to 10 minutes.
11. Allow the pot to cook the mixture until the timer goes off.
12. Turn off the pot & press "Cancel."
13. Now allow the built up pressure to vent out naturally; it will take 5 to 10 minutes to completely release inside pressure.
14. One thing remains to be done. Open its lid and transfer the cooked mixture into serving container/containers.
15. Finally serve warm!

Prep Time: 10 to 15 min.

Cooking Time: 15 to 20 min.

Number of Servings: 3 to 4

Vintage overload...

Nutritional information:

Calories – 324

Fat – 9.3g

Carbohydrates – 19.5g

Fiber – 2g

Protein – 42.3g

Titanic Tomato Chicken Stew

Wizard of all recipes.

Ingredients:

- 1 tablespoon sugar
- 3 ounces sweet potato
- About 1.5 teaspoon salt
- 1 pound boneless chicken breast
- 1 tablespoon oregano
- 1 teaspoon cilantro
- 2 tablespoons olive oil
- About 1.5 teaspoon fresh ginger
- 2 carrots

- 3 red onion
- 3 ounces scallions
- 5 ounces shallot
- About 1.5 tablespoon ground black pepper
- 1/2 cup cream
- 1/2 cup tomato juice
- 3 cups chicken stock

Directions:

1. First of all, please make sure you've all the ingredients available. Combine the tomato juice with the salt, cilantro, oregano, ground black pepper, & cream together in a mixing bowl and stir.
2. Now peel the onions, sweet potato, and carrots.
3. Chop the vegetables into medium-sized pieces.
4. This step is important. Set the Instant Pot to "Sauté" mode.
5. Place the chopped vegetables into the Instant Pot and sprinkle them with the olive oil. Sauté the vegetables for about 5 to 10 minutes.
6. Then add the tomato juice mixture and stir. Chop the shallot & scallions.
7. Add the chopped ingredients into the Instant Pot.
8. Now chop the boneless chicken breast roughly & add it into the Instant Pot, then add the chicken stock.
9. Stir well using a spoon and close the Instant Pot lid.
10. One thing remains to be done. Cook the dish on "Meat/Stew" mode for about 30 to 35 minutes.
11. Finally when the stew is cooked, remove it from the Instant Pot & transfer it to serving bowls.

Prep time: 15 to 20 minutes

Cooking time: 35 to 40 minutes

Servings: 8 to 9

Another fantastic recipe for you guys…

Nutritional information:

Calories 349

Fat 19.1

Fiber 5

Carbs 34.85

Protein 11

Rich Chicken Salsa.

For those who're ultra fantastic.

Ingredients:

- 16 oz. of salsa verde
- 1 tsp. smoked paprika
- About 1.5 tsp. cumin
- 1 tsp. salt
- 2 and 1/2 lb. of boneless chicken breasts

Directions:

1. First of all, please make sure you've all the ingredients available. Throw everything into your Instant Pot pressure cooker.
2. Now select "Manual" & then 25 to 30 minutes at "High" pressure.
3. When the timer goes off; quick-release the pressure.
4. One thing remains to be done. Carefully open the cooker & shred the chicken.
5. Finally serve & enjoy.

Servings: 6 to 8

Prep + Cook Time: 25 to 30 minutes

Simple yet tasty recipe.

Nutritional information:

Calories:- 340

Fat:- 7

Fiber:- 0

Carbs:- 6

Protein:- 59

Elegant Orange Spice Chicken

Simple recipe for you...

Ingredients:

- 2 tablespoons vegetable oil
- 4 green onions and orange zest
- About 2.5 garlic heads (Minced)
- 1 cup tomato sauce
- Salt and pepper to taste
- 1 cup orange juice
- 1/4 cup soy sauce
- About 4.5 tablespoons corn starch
- 1/4 cup granulated sugar
- 2 lb chicken breast cut into two-inch pieces
- 1/4 cup brown sugar

Directions:

1. First of all, please make sure you've all the ingredients available. Dry the chicken pieces with a paper towel.
2. Now add oil and chicken to the pot of the cooker.
3. Press the 'sauté' key, & cook the chicken properly on a medium-high heat for about 2 to 5 minutes, stirring constantly.
4. This step is important. When the chicken turns golden brown, add the rest of the ingredients to the pot.
5. Then mix all the ingredients well.
6. Cover and lock the cooker lid.
7. Select the 'poultry' option and set the timer for about 5 to 10 minutes.
8. Now after the completion beep, use 'natural release' to vent the steam for about 10 to 15 minutes. Then open the lid.

9. Mix the corn-starch with the orange juice in a separate bowl and add it to the pot.
10. Then select the 'sauté' function & cook the chicken properly in the sauce for about 5 to 10 minutes.
11. One thing remains to be done. Stir constantly until it thickens.
12. Finally garnish with chopped green onions & orange zest on top.

Serves: 6 to 7

Prep time: 15 to 20 minutes

Cooking time: 15 to 20 minutes

Delightful…

Nutritional information:

Calories: 818

Carbohydrate: 23.7g

Protein: 128.2g

Fat: 19.6g

Sugar: 19.6g

Sodium: 1120g

Wonderful Chicken And Potatoes Dish

Like never before…

Ingredients:

- 2 pounds chicken thighs, skinless and boneless
- Salt and black pepper to the taste
- 3/4 cup chicken stock
- 1/4 cup lemon juice
- About 2.5 tablespoons Italian seasoning
- About 2 pounds red potatoes, peeled and cut into quarters
- 2 tablespoons olive oil
- About 3.5 tablespoons Dijon mustard

Directions:

1. First of all, please make sure you've all the ingredients available. Now set your instant pot on sauté mode, add the oil, heat it up, add chicken thighs, salt and pepper, stir & brown for about 2 to 5 minutes.
2. One thing remains to be done. In a bowl, mix stock with mustard, Italian seasoning and lemon juice, stir well, pour over chicken, also add potatoes, cover and cook properly on High for about 15 to 20 minutes.
3. Finally divide among plates and serve. Enjoy!

Preparation time: 15 to 20 minutes

Cooking time: 15 to 20 minutes

Servings: 4 to 6

Worth it…

Nutritional information:

Calories 190

Fat 6

Fiber 3.3

Carbs 23

Protein 18

Quick Spicy Chicken Curry

My sister makes it every now & then.

Ingredients:

- 3 tbsp flour
- 1 tbsp vegetable oil
- About 2.5 tsp ground coriander
- 14 oz can tomatoes (Chopped)
- 2 tsp garam masala
- 2 tsp turmeric
- 2 green chilies (Chopped)
- About 2.5 tsp ground cumin
- 1 tsp ginger (Grated)
- 2 onion (Chopped)
- 1/2 lemon juice
- 4 garlic cloves, crushed
- 4 chicken thighs, boneless and cut into chunks

Directions:

1. First of all, please make sure you've all the ingredients available. Now please use the "Slow Cooker" setting on your Instant Pot.
2. Now add ginger, garlic, chilies, & onion into the blender and blend until smooth.
3. Now quickly heat oil in the pan over medium heat.
4. This step is important. Add blended puree into the pan & sauté for about 2 to 5 minutes.
5. Then add spices and sauté for about 2 to 5 minutes.
6. Add flour and tomatoes into the pan and stir well.
7. Refill tomato can halfway with water & adds in the pan. Stir well.
8. Now add chicken into the Instant Pot and season with pepper & salt.
9. Pour pan mixture over the chicken with lemon juice.
10. One thing remains to be done. Cover and cook properly on low for about 5 to 6 hours.
11. Finally serve & enjoy.

Total Time: 6 hours 20 to 25 minutes

Serves: 4 to 6

For a eternal experience.

Nutritional information:

Calories 387

Fat 14.8 g

Carbohydrates 17.3 g

Sugar 6 g

Protein 44.9 g

Cholesterol 130 mg

Awesome Eggplant Thai Style Chicken

Some things never fail you.

Ingredients:

- 6 boneless, skinless chicken thighs, make small pieces
- About 1.5 tablespoon oil
- 1 can coconut milk
- 3 tablespoons red curry paste
- 6 basil leaves, julienned
- About 2.5 tablespoons sugar
- 12 eggplants, make halves
- 1/2 cup chicken stock
- 2 tablespoons fish sauce

Directions:

1. First of all, please make sure you've all the ingredients available. Place your Instant Pot on a flat kitchen surface; plug it & turn it on.
2. Now to start making the recipe, press "Sauté" button.

3. Add the curry paste, chicken and 2 tablespoons of coconut milk; cook properly for about 2 to 5 minutes to soften the ingredients.
4. This step is important. Now add the fish sauce, eggplants, the rest of the coconut milk and stock.
5. Then carefully close its lid & firmly lock it. Then after, seal the valve too.
6. To start making the recipe, press "Manual" button. Now you have to set cooking time; set the timer for about 5 to 10 minutes.
7. Allow the pot to cook the mixture until the timer goes off.
8. Now turn off the pot & press "Cancel."
9. Allow the built up pressure to vent out naturally; it will take 5 to 10 minutes to completely release inside pressure.
10. One thing remains to be done. Open its lid & transfer the cooked mixture into serving container/containers.
11. Finally top with basil leaves. Serve with your favorite rice or salad.

Prep Time: 5 to 10 min.

Cooking Time: 10 to 15 min.

Number of Servings: 5 to 6

Mushroom fries bring back a lot of memories.

Nutritional information:

Calories - 388

Fat – 13g

Carbohydrates – 55.2g

Fiber – 25g

Protein – 13g

Legendary Shredded Chicken

Yeah, you can make it in your free time…

Ingredients:

- 1 tablespoon sugar
- 1 teaspoon turmeric
- About 1.5 teaspoon ground black pepper
- 1 teaspoon olive oil
- 3 garlic cloves
- 2 cups water
- 1 ounces bay leaf
- 1 teaspoon salt
- 1 tablespoon basil
- About 1.5 tablespoon butter
- 1/2 cup cream
- 1 pound chicken breast, boneless

Directions:

1. First of all, please make sure you've all the ingredients available. Set the Instant Pot to "Pressure" mode.
2. Now pour water into the Instant Pot & add the chicken breast.
3. Add the bay leaf. Close the lid and cook properly for about 10 to 15 minutes.
4. This step is important. When the cooking time ends, release the remaining pressure & open the Instant Pot lid.
5. Then transfer the chicken breast in a mixing bowl & shred it.
6. Sprinkle the shredded chicken with the sugar, ground black pepper, basil, salt, butter, cream, and turmeric and stir well.
7. Peel the garlic cloves and mince them.
8. Now spray the Instant Pot with the olive oil inside & transfer the shredded chicken in Instant Pot.
9. One thing remains to be done. Cook the dish properly on "Sauté" mode for about 10 to 15 minutes.
10. Finally when the dish is cooked, transfer it to a serving plate.

Prep time: 10 to 15 minutes

Cooking time: 20 to 25 minutes

Servings: 7 to 8

Supremacy defined!!

Nutritional information:

Calories 188

Fat 12

Fiber 1

Carbs 6.14

Protein 15

Excellent Italian Chicken Thighs.

I am actually popular among my friends for eating this one a lot.

Ingredients:

- 2 medium-sized; chopped carrots
- Salt to taste
- 1/2 lb. stemmed and quartered cremini mushrooms
- 2 cups. cherry tomatoes
- 3 smashed garlic cloves
- 1/4 cup. chopped fresh Italian parsley
- About 1.5 chopped onion
- 1 tbsp. olive oil
- 1/2 cup. thinly-sliced fresh basil
- 1 tbsp. tomato paste
- About 1 tsp. black pepper
- 8 boneless; skinless chicken thighs
- 1/2 cup. pitted green olives

Directions:

1. First of all, please make sure you've all the ingredients available. Season the chicken thighs with salt.
2. Now on your Instant Pot; hit "Sauté" & pour in the olive oil.
3. When shiny; toss in the c mushrooms, carrots, onions and a little salt.

4. This step is important. Cook properly for about 2 to 5 minutes until soft.
5. Then add the smashed garlic & tomato paste and cook for another 30 seconds.
6. Last; add the cherry tomatoes, chicken thighs & olives.
7. Turn off "Sauté" before locking the pressure cooker.
8. Now hit "Manual" and choose 10 to 15 minutes on "High" Pressure
9. One thing remains to be done. When the beeper goes off; quick-release the pressure right away.
10. Finally take off the lid & season. Serve.

Servings: 6 to 8

Prep + Cook Time: 25 to 30 minutes

So, what's your opinion?

Nutritional information:

Calories:- 245

Fiber:- 3

Carbs:- 10

Protein:- 35

Grains And Beans

Lucky Boiled Kidney Beans

Something is new here!!

Ingredients:

- About 1 teaspoon salt
- 1 cup dried white kidney beans
- 6 cups water

Directions:

1. First of all, please make sure you've all the ingredients available. Now place all ingredients in the Instant Pot.
2. One thing remains to be done. Then close the lid & seal off the vent.
3. Finally press the Manual button & adjust the cooking time to about 40 to 45 minutes.

Serves: 2 to 4

Preparation Time: 2 to 5 minutes

Cooking Time: 40 to 45 minutes

A little work here but will be worth it.

Nutritional information:

Calories per serving: 56

Carbohydrates: 3.4g

Protein: 2.2g

Fat: 3.8g

Fiber: 0.1g

Vintage Spinach Chickpea Curry

Get ready to make it my way!!

Ingredients:

- 1 1/2 tablespoons cooking oil
- Fistful of chopped fresh cilantro
- 1/2 cup chopped onions
- About 1.5 bay leaf
- Salt, to taste
- 1/2 tablespoon grated garlic
- About 1/2 tablespoon grated ginger
- 1 cup chopped baby spinach
- 3/4 cup water
- 1 cup fresh tomato puree
- 1/2 green chili, finely chopped
- About 1.5 teaspoon chili powder
- 1/4 teaspoon turmeric
- 1/2 teaspoon coriander powder
- 1/2 cup raw chickpeas

Directions:

1. First of all, please make sure you've all the ingredients available. Next, quickly add oil and onions to the Instant Pot. "Sauté" for about 5 to 10 minutes.
2. Now stir ginger, garlic paste, green chili & bay leaf. Cook properly for about 2 to 5 minutes, then add all the spices.
3. Add chickpeas, tomato puree & water to the pot.

4. This step is important. Cover and secure the lid. Turn its pressure release handle to the sealing position.
5. Then cook on the "Manual" function with high pressure for about 15 to 20 minutes.
6. After the beep, do a Natural release for about 20 to 25 minutes.
7. One thing remains to be done. Stir in spinach and cook properly for about 2 to 5 minutes on the "Sauté" setting.
8. Finally serve hot with boiled white rice.

Serves: 4 to 5

Prep Time: 10 to 15 minutes

Cooking Time: 25 to 30 minutes

The best combo ever!!

Nutritional information:

Calories: 180

Carbohydrate: 25.3g

Protein: 6.7g

Fat: 7g

Sugar: 6.9g

Sodium: 79mg

Best Creamy Mushroom Risotto (Gluten-Free)

Awesome, isn't it?

Ingredients:

- 2 cups Portobello mushrooms (Sliced)
- 3 cups chicken broth
- 1/2 cup parmesan cheese, grated – please check the ingredients
- 1/2 cup white wine
- About 1.5 small onion (Diced)
- 1/2 tsp salt
- 2 garlic cloves
- 2 cups Arborio rice
- 2 tbsp unsalted butter – please check the ingredients
- About 1.5 tbsp dried basil

Directions:

1. First of all, please make sure you've all the ingredients available. Melt 2 tbsp of unsalted butter in your instant pot by pressing "Sauté" button, & sauté onion & mushrooms for about 2 to 5 minutes.
2. Now add Arborio rice and sauté for about 2 to 5 more minutes until translucent.
3. Carefully add the white wine, chicken broth, and basil, sprinkle with salt.
4. Then with a wooden spoon, stir the rice, carefully scraping the bottom, to make sure rice is not stuck on it.

5. One thing remains to be done. Secure the lid, select "Manual" & cook properly at high pressure for about 5 to 10 minutes.
6. Finally when the time is up, quickly release the pressure, remove the lid & serve the risotto with grated parmesan cheese on top.

Preparation time: 10 to 15 min

Cooking time: 10 to 15 min

Servings: 6 to 7

Luxury tasty dish for you!!

Nutritional information:

Calories: 482

Protein: 11g

Fats: 15g

Carbs: 48g

Nostalgic Raw-Buckwheat Porridge.

Simple yet fantastic!!

Ingredients:

- 1 banana; sliced
- Chopped nuts; optional
- About 1.5 tsp. ground cinnamon

- 1/2 tsp. vanilla
- 3 cups. rice milk
- 1/4 cup. raisins
- 1 cup. raw buckwheat groats

Directions:

1. First of all, please make sure you've all the ingredients available. Rinse the buckwheat & then put in the Instant Pot container.
2. Then add the rice milk, banana, raisins, vanilla and cinnamon.
3. Close the lid & make sure the valve is closed.
4. This step is important. Set to "Manual"; the pressure is "High"; & the timer to about 5 to 10 minutes.
5. Now when the timer beeps at the end of the cooking cycle, unplug the pot & let the pressure release naturally for about 20 to 25 minutes.
6. With a long handled spoon, stir the porridge.
7. One thing remains to be done. Divide the porridge between 4 bowls.
8. Finally add more milk into each serving to desired consistency. If desired; sprinkle with chopped nuts.

Servings: 4 to 5

Prep + Cook Time: 35 to 40 minutes

It is a brand new day…. Ever listened to this one!!

Nutritional information:

Calories:- 247

Fat:- 2.6

Fiber:- 4.4

Carbs:- 54.3

Protein:- 4.7

Mighty Black Eyed Peas And Ham

This never goes out of style.

Ingredients:

- 6 1/2 cups chicken stock
- 1-pound dried black-eyed peas
- 5 ounces ham, diced

Directions:

1. Place all ingredients in the Instant Pot.
2. Close the lid and seal off the vent.
3. Press the Manual button and adjust the cooking time to 30 minutes.

Serves: 10 to 12

Preparation Time: 2 to 5 minutes

Cooking Time: 30 to 35 minutes

Now be a legend!!

Nutritional information:

Calories per serving: 90

Carbohydrates: 9.1g

Protein: 7.6g

Fat: 2.4g

Fiber: 1.2g

King Sized Almond Risotto

Good days!!

Ingredients:

- 1/2 cup Arborio (short-grain Italian) rice
- 1/4 cup toasted almond flakes
- About 2.5 tablespoons agave syrup
- 1 teaspoon vanilla extract
- 2 cups vanilla almond milk

Directions:

1. First of all, please make sure you've all the ingredients available. Now simply add all the ingredients to the Instant Pot.
2. Now cover and secure the lid. Turn its pressure release handle to the sealing position.
3. Cook on the "Manual" function with high pressure for about 5 to 10 minutes.
4. One thing remains to be done. Then after the beep, do a Natural release for about 20 to 25 minutes.

5. Finally garnish with almond flakes & serve.
6. I am interested!!

Serves: 3 to 4

Prep Time: 10 to 15 minutes

Cooking Time: 5 to 10 minutes

I am interested!!

Nutritional information:

Calories: 116

Carbohydrate: 22.5g

Protein: 2g

Fat: 2.1g

Sugar: 0.2g

Sodium: 82mg

Crazy Truffle Oil Risotto (Gluten-Free)

Now that's something!!

Ingredients:

- 2 cups button mushrooms (Sliced)
- About 6.5 tsp truffle oil
- 3 cups water
- 1/2 cup white wine

- 1 small onion (Diced)
- 1/2 cup parmesan cheese, grated – please check the ingredients
- 2 garlic cloves
- About 2.5 tbsp unsalted butter – please check the ingredients
- 2 cups Arborio rice
- 1/2 tsp salt

Directions:

1. First of all, please make sure you've all the ingredients available. Melt 2 tbsp of unsalted butter in your instant pot by pressing "Sauté" button, & sauté onion and button mushrooms for about 2 to 5 minutes.
2. Now add Arborio rice and saute for about 2 to 5 more minutes until translucent.
3. This step is important. Carefully add the water and white wine, sprinkle with salt.
4. Then with a wooden spoon, stir the rice, carefully scraping the bottom, to make sure rice is not stuck on it.
5. One thing remains to be done. Secure the lid, select "Manual" & cook properly at high pressure for about 5 to 10 minutes.
6. Finally when the time is up, quickly release the pressure, remove the lid & serve the risotto with grated parmesan cheese and truffle oil on top (1tsp for each serving is enough).

Preparation time: 10 to 15 min

Cooking time: 10 to 15 min

Servings: 6 to 7

Can you make it? Yes, why not?

Nutritional information:

Calories: 375

Protein: 9g

Fats: 13g

Carbs: 85g

Pinnacle Banana And Steel Cut Oatmeal.

Life of a legend begins here.

Ingredients:

- 2 cups. steel cut oatmeal
- 1/4 cup. honey
- About 1.5 tsp. cinnamon
- 1 tsp. vanilla
- 1/4 tsp. salt
- 1/4 tsp. nutmeg
- 3 and 1/3 cups. water
- About 2.5 ripe bananas; mashed
- 1/2 cup. walnuts (Chopped)

Directions:

1. First of all, please make sure you've all the ingredients available. With a potato masher or a fork; mash the bananas at the bottom of the Instant Pot container.
2. Now add the oats, cinnamon, water, nutmeg, vanilla and salt; stir to combine.
3. This step is important. Close the lid & make sure the valve is closed.
4. Then set the pot to "Porridge" & the timer to about 10 to 15 minutes.
5. When the timer beeps; let the pressure release for about 10 to 15 minutes naturally.
6. One thing remains to be done. Stir in the walnuts and honey.
7. Finally serve warm & enjoy!

Servings: 4 to 5

Prep + Cook Time: 25 to 30 minutes

Funny but definitely yummy!!

Nutritional information:

Calories:- 374

Fat:- 12.1

Fiber:- 7.1

Carbs: - 61

Protein:- 9.9

Perfect Spiced Black Beans

Something is definitely different.

Ingredients:

- 1-pound dry black beans, rinsed
- About 1 teaspoon paprika
- 5 1/2 cups water
- 1/2 teaspoon cumin
- About 1 teaspoon garlic powder
- 1/2 teaspoon coriander
- 2 1/2 tablespoon vegetable bullion

Directions:

1. First of all, please make sure you've all the ingredients available. Now place all ingredients in the Instant Pot.
2. One thing remains to be done. Then close the lid & seal off the vents.
3. Finally press the Manual button & adjust the cooking time to about 30 to 35 minutes.

Serves: 12 to 13

Preparation Time: 2 to 5 minutes

Cooking Time: 30 to 35 minutes

This is epic. Take a look!!

Nutritional information:

Calories per serving: 74

Carbohydrates: 9.4g

Protein: 3.1g

Fat: 3g

Fiber: 3.2g

Dashing Spinach Lentils Stew

Dreams are good!! So dream about this one or else make it...

Ingredients:

- 1 1/2 tablespoons cooking oil
- 1/2 cup fresh cilantro
- 1/2 cup chopped onions
- About 1.5 bay leaf
- Salt, to taste
- 1/2 tablespoon grated garlic
- 1/4 tablespoon grated ginger
- 1 cup chopped baby spinach
- 3/4 cup water
- 1 cup fresh tomato puree
- About 1.5 teaspoon chili powder
- 1/2 green chili, finely chopped
- 1/4 teaspoon turmeric
- 1/2 teaspoon coriander powder
- 1/2 cup raw lentils

Directions:

1. First of all, please make sure you've all the ingredients available. Add the oil and onions to the Instant Pot. "Sauté" for about 5 to 10 minutes.
2. Now stir ginger, garlic paste and bay leaf.
3. Cook properly for about 2 minutes, then add all the spices.
4. This step is important. Add lentils, tomato puree & water to the pot.
5. Cover and secure the lid. Turn its pressure release handle to the sealing position.
6. Then cook on the "Manual" function with high pressure for about 15 to 20 minutes.
7. After the beep, do a Natural release for about 20 to 25 minutes.
8. One thing remains to be done. Stir in spinach and cook properly for about 2 to 5 minutes on the "Sauté" setting.
9. Finally serve hot with boiled white rice.

Serves: 4 to 5

Prep Time: 10 to 15 minutes

Cooking Time: 25 to 30 minutes

Freshness loaded!!

Nutritional information:

Calories: 169

Carbohydrate: 23.2g

Protein: 7.9g

Fat: 5.7g

Sugar: 4.4g

Sodium: 75mg

Vegetables And Side Dishes

Crazy Pinto Beans

Super awesome plus unique!!

Ingredients:

- Onion1, chopped
- Sea salt1 1/2 tsp.
- Garlic4 cloves, minced
- Pepper1
- Oregano 1 tbsp.
- Tomato1/2, chopped
- Chili powder1 tbsp.
- Pinto beans1lb.
- Cumin2 tbsp.

Directions:

1. First of all, please make sure you've all the ingredients available. Take a large bowl & add the beans. Rinse thoroughly.
2. Then cover with water to soak & leave for several hours.
3. Drain the water and put the beans in the pot with the remaining ingredients. Stir to mix.

4. One thing remains to be done. Close the lid and cook using the chili function for about 20 to 25 minutes. Allow to depressurize naturally.
5. Finally serve with cilantro leaves.

Overall cooking time: 20 to 25 min

Servings: 8 to 9

Iconic recipe of my list!!

Nutritional information:

Calories: 230

Fat: 10g

Carbs: 25g

Protein: 10g

Pinnacle Cucumber Quinoa Salad

Well it is a Grandma's recipe!!

Ingredients:

- 3/4 cup water
- About 1/2 teaspoon salt
- 2 tablespoons chopped basil
- 1/2 carrot, peeled and shredded
- 1/2 cucumber (Chopped)
- 1/2 cup frozen edamame, thawed

- 1/4 cup freshly chopped cilantro
- About 3.5 green onions (Chopped)
- 1 cup shredded red cabbage
- 1/2 tablespoon soy sauce
- 1/2 cup peanuts (Chopped)
- About 1.5 tablespoon lime juice
- 2 tablespoons sugar
- pinch of red pepper flakes
- 1 tablespoon vegetable oil
- 1 tablespoon freshly grated ginger
- 1 tablespoon sesame oil
- 1/2 cup quinoa (Rinsed)

Directions:

1. First of all, please make sure you've all the ingredients available. Add the quinoa, salt, & water to the Instant Pot.
2. Now quickly secure the lid and select the "Manual" function with high pressure for about 2 minutes.
3. After the beep, do a quick release & remove the lid.
4. Then meanwhile, add the remaining ingredients to a bowl & mix well.
5. One thing remains to be done. Add the cooked quinoa to the prepared mixture & mix well.
6. Finally serve as a salad.

Serves: 4 to 5

Prep Time: 10 to 15 minutes

Cooking Time: 2 to 5 minutes

Happiness has finally arrived!!

Nutritional information:

Calories: 320

Carbohydrate: 31.2g

Protein: 12.1g

Fat: 18.5g

Sugar: 9.1g

Sodium: 279mg

Perfect Artichoke Hearts

Whenever you want a great recipe!!

Ingredients:

- Salt and black pepper to the taste
- 2 garlic cloves (Minced)
- About 2.5 tablespoons lemon juice
- 1/4 cup extra virgin olive oil
- 2 cups water
- About 2.5 teaspoons balsamic vinegar
- 4 big artichokes, washed, stems and petal tips cut off
- 1 teaspoon oregano

Directions:

1. First of all, please make sure you've all the ingredients available. Add 2 cups water to your instant pot, add steamer basket, add artichokes inside, cover & cook properly on High for about 5 to 10 minutes.
2. Now in a bowl, mix lemon juice with vinegar, pepper, oil, salt, garlic and oregano and stir very well.
3. Transfer artichokes to a plate, halve them, take out the hearts & arrange them on a platter.
4. One thing remains to be done. Then drizzle the vinaigrette over artichokes & leave them aside for about 30 to 35 minutes.
5. Finally clean your instant pot, set it on sauté mode, heat it up, add artichokes, cook properly for about 2 to 5 minutes on each side & serve them warm. Enjoy!

Preparation time: 10 to 15 minutes

Cooking time: 40 to 45 minutes

Servings: 4 to 5

How is it? Only one way to find out…

Nutritional information:

Calories 120

Fat 2

Fiber 1

Carbs 1

Protein 4

Dashing Brussels Sprouts

I can eat them all day!!

Ingredients:

- Olive oil 2.5 tbsp.
- Pine nuts 1/4 cup
- Salt and pepper 1 pinch each
- Brussels sprouts 1lb.

Directions:

1. First of all, please make sure you've all the ingredients available. First, take your instant pot trivet, set inside the pot, & then place the steamer basket.
2. Then add one cup of water and then the Brussels sprouts.
3. One thing remains to be done. Fasten the lid and set the time to about 2 to 5 minutes at high pressure.
4. Finally season with pepper, pine nuts, salt, olive oil, etc.

Overall cooking time: 15 to 20 min

Servings: 4 to 6

Different take on this one…

Nutritional information:

Calories: 67

Fat: 5g,

Carbs: 5.2g

Protein: 2g

Reliable Frijoles Borrachos (Mexican "Drunken Beans")

Yeah, you can make it in your free time…

Ingredients:

- 1 green bell pepper (Diced)
- 1 lime, cut into wedges
- About 1.5 tablespoon vegetable oil
- 4 cloves garlic (Minced)
- 1 teaspoon cumin
- 1 pound dry Pinto beans (rinsed, drained)
- 8 cups vegetable stock or water
- 1 can (28 ounces) diced stewed tomatoes
- 3 whole dried bay leaves
- 1 can (12 ounces) Mexican beer
- 1 can (4 ounces) diced jalapenos (drained)
- About 1.5 tablespoon salt, plus more to taste
- 1 teaspoon ground chipotle chili pepper
- 2 teaspoons dried oregano
- About 1 1/2 teaspoons freshly ground black pepper, plus more to taste
- Salt, to taste

- 1 white onion (diced)

Directions:

1. First of all, please make sure you've all the ingredients available. In Instant Pot on sauté setting, cook onion & bell pepper in oil until softened, about 5 to 10 minutes.
2. Now add garlic and cook about 2 minutes more.
3. This step is important. Add beans, vegetable stock, beer, undrained tomatoes, jalapenos, salt, chipotle pepper, oregano, black pepper, bay leaves and cumin to pot and mix thoroughly.
4. Then secure pot lid, close pressure valve and cook on bean/chili setting for about 35 to 40 minutes.
5. When cooking time ends, let pressure release naturally.
6. Remove bay leaves, stir beans & season to taste with salt and pepper.
7. One thing remains to be done. If desired, mash beans with a fork to thicken the cooking juices.
8. Finally garnish beans with lime wedges to serve. Enjoy!

Serves: 8 to 9

Preparation time: 10 to 15 minutes

Cooking time: 40 to 45 minutes

Supremacy defined!!

Nutritional information:

Calories: 156

Total Fat: 3g

Saturated Fat: 1g

Protein: 8g

Carbs: 29g

Fiber: 18g

Sugar: 4g

Charming Coconut & Quinoa Curry (Gluten-Free)

A fine recipe, it just works.

Ingredients:

- 2 cups cooked chickpeas, drained and rinsed
- About 1.5 tsp chili flakes
- 2 cups full fat coconut milk
- 1 tbsp ginger root, peeled and grated
- 2 garlic cloves, minced
- About 1.5 tsp turmeric powder
- 1/4 cup quinoa
- 3 cups potato, peeled and chopped
- 1 small onion (Diced)
- 2 cups broccoli florets
- 2 cups diced tomato

Directions:

1. First of all, please make sure you've all the ingredients available. Put 1 cup of still water into the instant pot & then add all other ingredients, stir well.
2. Now select "Slow cooker" mode and set the timer for about 3 to 4 hours.
3. One thing remains to be done. The curry should be thick.
4. Finally when the time is up, carefully remove the lid, stir your curry with a wooden spatula & serve immediately.

Preparation time: 20 to 25 min

Cooking time: 4h

Servings: 8 to 9

Yummy, definitely yummy.

Nutritional information:

Calories: 510

Protein: 13g

Fats: 32g

Carbs: 50g

Energetic Pepper Soup

Don't wait, eat it!!

Ingredients:

- 1 white onion (Chopped)
- Pinch of black pepper
- About 1.5 garlic clove (Minced)
- Pinch of salt
- 1 cup red bell pepper (Diced)
- 1 fresh jalapeno pepper (Diced)
- 1 cup water
- 1 cup summer squash (Diced)
- 1 cup zucchini, diced
- About 1 tsp. cayenne powder
- 2 cups vegetable stock
- 1/2 tsp. sweet paprika powder
- 1/2 tsp. coriander powder
- 2 Tbsp. olive oil

Directions:

1. First of all, please make sure you've all the ingredients available. Pour olive oil into the Instant Pot Pressure Cooker.
2. Now press the "saute" button.
3. Saute onion and garlic for about 2 to 5 minutes or until limp and fragrant.
4. This step is important. Add in red bell pepper, summer squash, jalapeno pepper, zucchini, sweet paprika powder, cayenne powder, & coriander powder. Pour vegetable stock and water.
5. Then season with salt and pepper.
6. Lock the lid in place. Press the "manual" button & cook properly for about 5 to 10 minutes.
7. When the beep sounds, Choose the Quick Pressure Release.

8. Now this will depressurize for about 5 to 10 minutes. Remove the lid.
9. One thing remains to be done. Turn off the crockpot.
10. Finally adjust seasoning according to your preferred taste. Serve.

Serves: 3 to 4

RECOMMENDED SERVING SIZE: 1 bowl

Just make it once and you will keep making it!!

Nutritional information:

Calories - 100

Carbohydrates – 16 grams

Fat – 9 grams

Protein - 5 grams

Funny Saucy Baked Beans

Good luck!!

Ingredients:

- 1/2 cup bacon (Diced)

- 1/2 cup water
- 1/4 medium onion (Diced)
- About 1 teaspoon sea salt
- 1/2 teaspoon pepper
- 1/2 cup chicken stock
- 1/2 teaspoon dry mustard
- About 1 tablespoon Worcestershire sauce
- 3 tablespoons molasses
- 1/2 tablespoon balsamic vinegar
- 1 tablespoon tomato paste
- 1 cup dry Navy beans (soaked for 8 hours and rinsed)
- 3 tablespoons dark brown sugar

Directions:

1. First of all, please make sure you've all the ingredients available. Now please add the bacon to the Instant Pot and "Sauté" for about 2 to 5 minutes until it turns crispy.
2. Now remove the bacon and add onions to cook properly for about 5 to 10 minutes with occasional stirring.
3. This step is important. Stir in all the remaining ingredients.
4. Then secure the lid and select the "Bean" function with 30 to 35 minutes cooking time.
5. One thing remains to be done. After the beep, do a Natural release for about 10 to 15 minutes, then remove the lid.
6. Finally stir in cooked bacon and cook properly for another 10 to 15 minutes on "Sauté" setting.

Serves: 4 to 5

Prep time: 10 to 15 minutes

Cooking time: 1 hour

Oh yeah!!

Nutritional information:

Calories: 269

Carbohydrate: 51.7g

Protein: 13g

Fat: 2g

Sugar: 18.2g

Sodium: 420mg

Awesome Artichokes And Spinach Dip

Stupidly simple...

Ingredients:

- 8 ounces cream cheese
- About 1.5 teaspoon onion powder
- 16 ounces parmesan cheese (Grated)
- 1/2 cup mayonnaise
- 10 ounces spinach
- 1/2 cup chicken stock
- About 3.5 garlic cloves (Minced)
- 8 ounces mozzarella (Shredded)
- 14 ounces canned artichoke hearts
- 1/2 cup sour cream

Directions:

1. First of all, please make sure you've all the ingredients available. Now in your instant pot, mix artichokes with stock, garlic, spinach, sour cream, cream cheese, onion powder and mayo, stir, cover & cook properly on High for about 5 to 10 minutes.
2. Finally add mozzarella and parmesan, stir well, transfer to a bowl & serve with corn chips on the side. Enjoy!

Preparation time: 10 to 15 minutes

Cooking time: 5 to 10 minutes

Servings: 6 to 7

Be unique, be extraordinary…

Nutritional information:

Calories 288

Fat 20

Fiber 0

Carbs 8

Protein 15

Lunch

Nostalgic Dal

Amazing cooking starts here…

Ingredients:

- 1/2 cup fennel
- 1 teaspoon cumin
- 1 teaspoon turmeric
- 1 teaspoon cilantro
- 3 medium tomatoes
- 1 teaspoon salt
- 4 cups water
- 2 white onions
- 1/2 tablespoon ground black pepper
- 2 cups lentils

Directions:

1. First of all, please make sure you've all the ingredients available. Place the lentils in the Instant Pot. Chop the fennel & add it in the Instant Pot.
2. Now combine the cumin, cilantro, salt, ground black pepper, & oregano together. Blend the mixture well.
3. This step is important. Peel the white onions & dice them. Chop the tomatoes.

4. Then combine the diced onions & chopped tomatoes together in the Instant Pot. Sprinkle it with the spice mixture.
5. Add water and blend well carefully. Close the Instant Pot lid, and set the Instant Pot mode to "Steam." Cook properly for about 30 to 35 minutes.
6. One thing remains to be done. When the dal is cooked, let cooked, let the dish rest briefly.
7. Finally transfer it to a serving bowl.

Prep time: 10 to 15 minutes

Cooking time: 30 to 35 minutes

Servings: 5 to 6

Don't forget this one…

Nutritional information:

Calories 72

Fat 0.5

fiber 3

carbs 15.52

protein 4

Best Roasted Beef

Sizzle your taste buds...

Ingredients:

- About 1.5 Tbsp. of vegetable oil
- Lime wedges
- 1 large chopped onion
- About 1 and 1/2 cup of beef broth or water
- 1 Pinch of ground pepper
- About 3.5 bay leaves
- 3 and 1/2 lb. of Beef Chuck
- 1 pinch of salt

Directions:

1. First of all, please make sure you've all the ingredients available. Pat your roast dry and season it with salt & pepper
2. Now pour the oil in your Instant Pot and press the button sauté.
3. Add the onion and cook it properly for about 2 to 5 minutes.
4. This step is important. Add the beef meat and pour 1 cup of water.
5. Then close the lid of the Instant Pot * set at high pressure for about 15 to 20 minutes.
6. When the timer beeps, quick release the pressure and let the meat boil for about 20 to 25 more minutes
7. Now please check if the meat is cooked with a toothpick
8. Now add the meat & press sauté for about 5 to 10 minutes
9. Remove your roasted meat to a serving dish.

10. One thing remains to be done. Serve with onion & lime wedges
11. Finally you can also thicken the juices in your Instant Pot by simmering with the water & the flour or the corn starch in order to prepare the gravy.

Time: 35 to 40 minutes

Servings: 2 to 3

Legends are born in...

Nutritional information:

Calories 53g

Fats 4.2g

Cholesterol 86mg

Total Carbohydrates 0.0g

Protein 1.8g

Vintage Risotto

Jaw dropping!!

Ingredients:

- 1 red onion
- 1/2 teaspoon coriander
- About 1.5 teaspoon turmeric
- 8 ounces potatoes
- 1 tablespoon tomato paste
- 4 cups chicken stock
- 1 teaspoon salt
- 1 teaspoon basil
- About 2.5 tablespoons olive oil
- 1/2 tablespoon paprika
- 1 cup rice
- 1 teaspoon cilantro

Directions:

1. First of all, please make sure you've all the ingredients available. Peel the onion and dice it. Place the diced onion in the Instant Pot.
2. Then add olive oil, rice, & salt. Sauté the mixture for about 2 to 5 minutes, stirring frequently. Peel the potatoes & grate it.
3. This step is important. Add the grated potatoes to the sautéed mixture & mix well.
4. Turmeric, chicken stock, paprika, tomato paste, cilantro, basil, and coriander. Blend the mixture well using a wooden spoon.
5. Now set the Instant Pot mode to "Pressure" & close the lid. Cook for about 10 to 15 minutes.
6. One thing remains to be done. When the cooking time ends, remove the risotto from the Instant Pot to prevent the overcooking of the rice.

7. Finally leave the rice for about 15 to 20 minutes & then transfer it to serving bowls.

Prep time: 25 to 30 minutes

Cooking time: 10 to 15 minutes

Servings: 4 to 5

Speed defines it…

Nutritional information:

Calories 302

Fat 16

Fiber 9

Carbs 37.41

Protein 12

Lucky Beef Meat Loaf

Mystery with this recipe or rather a chemistry with it.

Ingredients:

- 3 Slices of bread
- 1/2 Cup of BBQ sauce

- About 2.5 lbs. of ground beef
- 8 Slices of bacon slices
- 3/4 Cup of grated Parmesan cheese
- 1 Teaspoon of salt
- 3 Beaten eggs
- About 1/2 Teaspoon of salt
- 1 Pinch of freshly ground black pepper
- 1/2 Cup of milk
- 2 Tbsp. of dried parsley

Directions:

1. First of all, please make sure you've all the ingredients available. In a deep mixing bowl, pour your milk over bread & set it aside to soak for a few minutes.
2. Then add the ground meat of beef, the Parmesan cheese, the salt, the black pepper, the parsley & the beaten eggs.
3. With your clean hands, combine the ingredients until they become very well – combined.
4. This step is important. Place a sling of tin foil to the shape of your meat & shape it into the form of a long bread loaf.
5. Now lay your bacon on top, & tuck it under the meatloaf too.
6. Spread around 1/4 cup of BBQ sauce just on the top of your bacon.
7. Then place the trivet in your Instant Pot & place your meatloaf above it; then close the lid of the Instant Pot and set at high pressure for twenty minutes
8. One thing remains to be done. When the timer beeps, turn off the Instant Pot & quick release the pressure.

9. Finally broil the meatloaf with the remaining quantity of BBQ sauce for around 5 to 10 minutes.

Time: 25 to 30 minutes

Servings: 5 to 7

Awesomeness fully loaded…

Nutritional information:

Calories 294g

Fats 17.4g

Cholesterol 114mg

Total Carbohydrates 9.4g

Protein 23.7g

Happy Warm Chicken Salad

Now the wait is over for hungry people.

Ingredients:

- 3 medium tomatoes
- 1/2 lemon
- 2 cucumber
- About 1.5 tablespoon olive oil
- 1 teaspoon salt
- 1 teaspoon cayenne pepper
- 1 pound chicken breast
- 3 ounces black olives
- About 1.5 teaspoon basil
- 1 tablespoon apple cider vinegar
- 5 ounces romaine lettuce
- 1 teaspoon ground black pepper

Directions:

1. First of all, please make sure you've all the ingredients available. Sprinkle the chicken breast with the basil, salt, apple cider vinegar, & cayenne pepper, and stir it carefully.
2. Now transfer the meat to the Instant Pot & close the lid.
3. Set the Instant Pot mode to "Poultry," and cook properly for about 30 to 35 minutes.
4. This step is important. Meanwhile, chop the lettuce roughly.
5. Then slice the olives and chop the cucumbers & tomatoes.
6. Combine the vegetables together in a mixing bowl. Sprinkle the dish with the olive oil. Squeeze the lemon juice.
7. Now when the chicken is cooked, remove it from the Instant Pot & let the meat rest briefly.
8. One thing remains to be done. Slice the chicken into medium pieces. Add the sliced meat in the mixing bowl.
9. Finally mix the salad using wooden spoons.

Prep time: 15 to 20 minutes

Cooking time: 30 to 35 minutes

Servings: 6 to 7

Magical, isn't it?

Nutritional information:

Calories 141

Fat 8.1

Fiber 2

Carbs 8.82

Protein 9

Great Potatoes With Ground Meat

Yeah, it is a vintage recipe.

Ingredients:

- 2 minced garlic cloves
- Freshly coriander (Chopped)
- About 2.5 Tbsp. of groundnut oil
- 1 and 1/2 cup of frozen peas
- 1 lb. of lean minced beef
- 1 Large potato
- 1 lb. of chopped tomatoes
- 1 teaspoon of ground coriander
- 1 Teaspoon of cumin

- 1 Cup of beef stock
- About 1.5 Teaspoon of chilli powder
- 1 teaspoon of turmeric
- 1/2 Tbsp. of Garam Masala
- 1 large red diced onion

Directions:

1. First of all, please make sure you've all the ingredients available. Pour 2 Tbsp. of vegetable oil in your Instant Pot
2. Now press sauté and add 1 large chopped onion together with the minced garlic cloves and cook properly for about 2 to 5 minutes.
3. Add 1 lb. of minced beef & the diced potato.
4. Add 1 teaspoon of the ground coriander & the cumin, the chilli powder and the turmeric.
5. This step is important. Add 1 tbsp. of the Garam Masala, & cook all of the ingredients together for around 2 to 5 minutes.
6. Then add the beef stock made of 1 lb. of diced tomatoes and 1 stock cube.
7. Season your ingredients with the salt & the ground pepper and closer the lid of the Instant Pot
8. Now set high pressure for about 10 to 15 minutes.
9. One thing remains to be done. When the timer beeps, quick release the pressure and add the frozen peas; then cook properly for about 5 to 10 minutes.
10. Finally serve your delicious lunch with fresh chopped coriander.

Time: 30 to 35 minutes

Servings: 4 to 5

Always the upper hand...

Nutritional information:

Calories 300g

Fats 10.3g

Cholesterol 80.7mg

Total Carbohydrates 18.5g

Protein 31.6g

Fantastic Aromatic Congee

Now you're happy...?

Ingredients:

- 1 teaspoon salt
- 1 teaspoon rosemary
- About 1.5 tablespoon oregano
- 1/2 teaspoon ground ginger
- 5 cups water

- 1 tablespoon butter
- 1/2 cup fresh dill
- 1 pound chicken fillet
- About 1.5 teaspoon turmeric
- 2 cups rice

Directions:

1. First of all, please make sure you've all the ingredients available. Combine the rice and water together & place the mixture in the Instant Pot.
2. Now add ground ginger and oregano. Chop the chicken fillet & add it in the Instant Pot too.
3. This step is important. Stir the mixture and close the lid.
4. Set the Instant Pot mode to "Pressure," and cook properly for about 30 to 35 minutes.
5. Then add butter, dill, turmeric, & rosemary. Stir the mixture gently.
6. Sauté the congee in the Instant Pot for about 10 to 15 minutes.
7. One thing remains to be done. When the cooking time ends, remove the congee from the Instant Pot & let it chill.
8. Finally serve the dish in individual bowls.

Prep time: 10 minutes

Cooking time: 40 minutes

Servings: 6

Classic style...

Nutritional information:

Calories 344

Fat 20.9

Fiber 10

Carbs 37.47

Protein 14

Delightful Butter Chicken

Arrive in style with this recipe.

Ingredients:

- 2 cups of diced tomatoes with its juice
- 1/4 Cup of minced cilantro
- 3 Seeded and chopped jalapeno peppers
- About 2.5 Tbsp. of peeled and chopped fresh ginger root
- 2 Tbsp. of water
- 1/2 Cup of unsalted butter
- 2 Teaspoons of ground cumin
- 2 Tbsp. of corn starch
- 1 Tbsp. of paprika
- About 2.5 Teaspoons of kosher salt
- 3/4 Cup of heavy cream
- 2 Teaspoons of ground roasted cumin seeds

- 3/4 Cup of Greek yogurt
- 2 Teaspoons of Garam Masala
- 9 boneless and skinless chicken thighs

Directions:

1. First of all, please make sure you've all the ingredients available. Cut the chicken into cubes or quarters. Put the tomatoes, the jalapeno & the ginger into a food processor and blend all of the ingredients.
2. Now add a little bit of butter to the Instant Pot, select the sauté function.
3. When the butter is completely melted, add the chicken & cook for 3 minutes.
4. This step is important. Remove the chicken into a bow and set it aside.
5. Add the ground cumin and the paprika to the butter into your Instant Pot and cook all together for about 2 minutes.
6. Then add the tomatoes, the salt, the cream, the yogurt & the chicken.
7. Stir and cover the lid of the Instant Pot; then set high pressure for around 5 to 10 minutes.
8. Now when the timer beeps, naturally release the pressure for around 10 to 15 minutes.
9. One thing remains to be done. Add the Garam Masala and the roasted cumin and combine the ingredients together; then press sauté to boil for about 2 to 5 minutes.
10. Finally serve and enjoy with rice & garnish with cilantro.

Time: 30 to 35 minutes

Servings: 4 to 5

Ironic in taste...

Nutritional information:

Calories 505.2g

Fats 22.3g

Cholesterol 17.5mg

Total Carbohydrates 16.4g

Protein 59.7g

Super Lentil Stew

Looking forward to this one!!

Ingredients:

- 5 cups beef stock
- 1/2 lemon
- About 1.5 teaspoon salt
- 1/2 teaspoon sugar
- 2 carrots
- 1 tablespoon sour cream
- About 1.5 tablespoon ground black pepper
- 2 cups lentils
- 1/4 cup thyme leaves

Directions:

1. First of all, please make sure you've all the ingredients available. Peel the carrots and chop them. Slice the lemon.
2. Then combine the salt, ground black pepper, sugar, & sour cream together in a mixing bowl.
3. This step is important. Chop the thyme leaves & add them to the spice mixture. Place the lentils in the Instant Pot.
4. Now add sliced lemon and beef stock. Add the spice mixture, & stir the lentils until you get a smooth mixture.
5. Next, quickly close the lid & then set the Instant Pot mode to "Pressure." Cook properly for about 30 to 35 minutes.
6. One thing remains to be done. When the dish is cooked, open the lid & stir the mixture well using a wooden spoon.
7. Finally transfer the stew to serving bowls & add additional salt, if desired, before serving.

Prep time: 15 to 20 minutes

Cooking time: 30 to 35 minutes

Servings: 6 to 7

Used to eat this one a lot.

Nutritional information:

Calories 71

Fat 0.6

Fiber 1

Carbs 11.77

Protein 7

Awesome Lamb With Black Beans

There it is.

Ingredients:

- 1 lb. of ground lamb
- 1 can of chopped and undrained green chillies
- 1/2 Cup of chopped onion
- 1 and 1/2 tbsp. of chilli powder
- 1 Can of chicken broth
- About 2.5 Teaspoons of cumin
- 1/2 Teaspoon of salt
- 1 can of undrained diced tomatoes
- 1/2 Teaspoon of cayenne
- 1 and 1/2 tbsp. of tomato paste
- About 2.5 Tbsp. of vegetable oil
- 2 cans of drained black beans

Directions:

1. First of all, please make sure you've all the ingredients available. Place your Instant Pot over a medium-high heat until.

2. Then pour 2 tbsp. of oil in the Instant Pot & when it becomes hot, add the lamb and the onion and press sauté for about 5 to 10 minutes.
3. Add the chilli powder and the rest of your ingredients; then close the lid of your Instant Pot & set at high pressure for around 20 to 25 minutes.
4. One thing remains to be done. When the timer beeps, quick release the pressure.
5. Finally serve & enjoy your lunch!

Time: 25 to 30 minutes

Servings: 5 to 8

Tasty dish just one step away!!

Nutritional information:

Calories 358.4g

Fats 18.5g

Cholesterol 55.2mg

Total Carbohydrates 28.5g

Protein 21.3g

Iconic Pasta Bolognese

I was waiting for this one.

Ingredients:

- 1 teaspoon olive oil
- About 1 tablespoon paprika
- 2 white onions
- 1 cup ground beef
- 1 teaspoon cilantro
- 3 tablespoons chives
- 1 teaspoon salt
- About 1.5 teaspoon turmeric
- 4 cups chicken stock
- 1/2 cup tomato sauce
- 8 ounces penne
- 2 tablespoons soy sauce

Directions:

1. First of all, please make sure you've all the ingredients available. Peel the onions and slice it. Place the sliced onions in the Instant Pot.
2. Now add ground beef, cilantro, salt, turmeric, and paprika.
3. Stir the mixture well & sauté it for about 2 to 5 minutes. Stir it gently.
4. This step is important. Remove the mixture from the Instant Pot & add soy sauce, tomato sauce, and chives.

5. Then sauté the mixture for about 2 to 5 minutes. Add the penne and chicken stock.
6. Add ground beef mixture and close the lid.
7. Now cook the dish on the instant mode to "Pressure" for about 5 to 10 minutes.
8. One thing remains to be done. When the dish is cooked, release the remaining pressure & open the lid.
9. Finally mix up the dish & transfer it to serving plates.

Prep time: 10 to 15 minutes

Cooking time: 15 to 20 minutes

Servings: 6 to 7

I know, this is amazing!!

Nutritional information:

Calories 245

Fat 10.2

Fiber 3

Carbs 21.96

Protein 15

Chicken And Beef

Quick Mouthwatering Steak.

Being rich is a plus point ?

Ingredients:

- About 2.5 tbsp. onion soup mix; dried
- 1/4 cups. apple cider vinegar
- 1/2 cups. olive oil
- 1 tbsp. Worcestershire sauce
- 2 lb. flank steak

Directions:

1. First of all, please make sure you've all the ingredients available. Press the "Sauté" key of the Instant Pot.
2. Now put the flank steak in the pot & cook each side until browned.
3. Add the vinegar, Worcestershire sauce, onion soup mix and olive oil.
4. This step is important. Press the "Cancel" key to stop the sauté function.
5. Then cover & lock the lid.
6. Press the "Meat/Stew" key; set the pressure to "High"; & set the timer for about 35 to 40 minutes.
7. One thing remains to be done. When the Instant Pot timer beeps; turn the steam valve to quick release the pressure.
8. Finally unlock & carefully open the lid. Serve!

Servings: 4 to 5

Prep + Cook Time: 45 to 50 minutes

Amazing cooking starts here…

Nutritional information:

Calories:- 684

Fat:- 44.1

Fiber:- 0

Carbs:- 5.5

Protein:- 63.6

Wonderful Instant Pot Roasted Chicken

Don't forget this one...

Ingredients:

- About 2.5 tbsp. flour, for dusting
- 1 cup chicken stock
- 2 lbs. whole chicken
- 2 sprigs rosemary leaves
- 2 tbsp. parsley
- 4 garlic cloves, crushed
- Pinch of salt
- About 4.5 tbsp. olive oil
- Pinch of pepper, to taste

Directions:

1. First of all, please make sure you've all the ingredients available. Combine rosemary sprigs & parsley in a bowl.
2. Now season with salt and pepper. Stir well.

3. Rub the mixture inside the chicken cavity.
4. Place garlic clove inside the cavity as well. Dust chicken with flour.
5. This step is important. Tie chicken wings & legs.
6. Then in the Instant Pot, pour olive oil. Press the "saute" button. Place chicken & cook until lightly seared.
7. Pour chicken stock & the remaining marinade.
8. Lock the lid in place. Press the high pressure & cook properly for about 25 to 30 minutes.
9. Now when the beep sounds, Choose Natural Pressure Release. Depressurizing would take 20 to 25 minutes.
10. Turn off the Instant Pot. Remove the lid.
11. Transfer to a platter. Tent chicken with aluminum foil.
12. Then put back into the Instant Pot. Pour remaining stock & cooking liquid.
13. One thing remains to be done. Reposition the lid and lock in place. Press the "pressure" button and cook properly for another 5 to 10 minutes.
14. Finally to serve, cut chicken into pieces. Pour sauce over chicken.

Serves: 4 to 6

Recommended Serving Size: 1 -2 chicken slices

Sizzle your taste buds...

Nutritional information:

Calories – 254

Carbohydrates – 0 gram

Fat – 9.92 grams

Protein – 38.73 grams

Elegant Lemon Olive Chicken

Legends are born in...

Ingredients:

- 1/2 teaspoon cumin
- 1 can pitted green olives
- About 1.5 teaspoon salt
- 1/2 teaspoon black pepper
- 1 cup chicken broth
- 1/2 cup butter (Melted)
- 4 chicken breasts, bones, and skin removed
- Juice of 1 lemon

Directions:

1. First of all, please make sure you've all the ingredients available. In a bowl, please season the chicken breasts with salt, cumin, and pepper.
2. Now press the Sauté button on the Instant Pot & place the chicken meat and butter.
3. This step is important. Brown all sides for about 2 to 5 minutes.
4. Then add the rest of the ingredients.
5. Close the lid & press the Poultry button.

6. One thing remains to be done. Adjust the cooking time for about 10 to 15 minutes.
7. Finally do quick pressure release.

Serves: 8 to 9

Preparation Time: 5 to 10 minutes

Cooking Time: 10 to 15 minutes

Jaw dropping!!

Nutritional information:

Calories per serving:401

Carbohydrates: 0.8g

Protein: 36.9g

Fat: 27g

Fiber: 0.2g

Rich Easy And Hearty Beef Stew

Speed defines it…

Ingredients:

- 1 bay leaf
- 1/2 tsp kosher salt
- About 1 tsp Worcestershire sauce
- 1 1/2 cups beef broth

- 1/2 tsp ground black pepper
- 2 carrots (Diced)
- 1 1/2 cup potatoes, peeled and diced
- 4 tbsp all purpose flour
- About 1 tsp garlic powder
- 1 tsp onion powder
- 1 lb beef stew meat, cut into 1-inch pieces

Directions:

1. First of all, please make sure you've all the ingredients available. Use the "Slow Cooker" setting on your Instant Pot.
2. Now add all-purpose flour, onion powder, garlic powder, black pepper, and salt into the large zip-lock bag & mix well.
3. Add meat pieces to the flour mixture & coat well.
4. This step is important. Place coated meat pieces in the slow cooker.
5. Then add carrots & potatoes over the meat.
6. Mix together Worcestershire sauce & beef broth and pour into the slow cooker. Top with bay leaf.
7. One thing remains to be done. Cover and cook properly on low for about 5 to 6 hours.
8. Finally discard bay leaf & serve.

Total Time: 6 hours 10 to 15 minutes

Serves: 2 to 4

Mystery with this recipe or rather a chemistry with it.

Nutritional information:

Calories 622

Fat 15.5 g

Carbohydrates 39 g

Sugar 5.7 g

Protein 76.8 g

Cholesterol 203 mg

Titanic Beef Bourguignon

Awesomeness fully loaded…

Ingredients:

- 1/2 pound bacon tips or rashers
- 1/2 cup beef broth or stock
- 5 carrots; medium-sized, cut into sticks
- 2 sweet potato; large white, peeled and cubed
- 2 cloves garlic; minced
- About 2.5 tbsp parsley; dried or fresh
- 1 tbsp maple syrup
- 2 tbsp thyme; dried or fresh
- 2 tsp ground black pepper
- About 1.5 tbsp avocado oil or olive oil
- 2 tsp rock salt
- 1 cup red wine
- 1 pound flank steak or stewing steak
- 1 red onion; large-sized, peeled and sliced

Directions:

1. First of all, please make sure you've all the ingredients available. Press the "Sauté" key of the Instant Pot.
2. Now put 1 tbsp. oil in the pot & heat.
3. Pat the beef dry & season with salt and pepper.
4. Working in batches, cook the beef properly in the pot until all sides are browned. Set aside.
5. This step is important. Slice the bacon into strips & put into the pot.
6. Then add the onions, Sauté until the onions are translucent & soft.
7. Return the browned beef in the pot.
8. Add the remaining ingredients.
9. Now press the "Cancel" key to stop the sauté function.
10. Cover & lock the lid.
11. Press the "Manual" key; set the pressure to "High"; and set the timer for about 30 to 35 minutes.
12. One thing remains to be done. When the Instant Pot timer beeps; turn the steam valve to "Venting" to quick release the pressure.
13. Finally unlock & carefully open the lid. Enjoy!

Servings: 4 to 5

Prep + Cook Time: 1 hour 15 to 20 minutes

Now the wait is over for hungry people.

Nutritional information:

Calories:- 701

Fat:- 34

Fiber:- 5.4

Carbs:- 30.1

Protein:- 55.7

Tasty Instant Pot Chicken Drumsticks

Magical, isn't it?

Ingredients:

- Pinch of salt
- 1 cup water
- Pinch of white pepper, to taste
- About 2.5 tsp. dry sand ginger
- 1/4 tsp. five spice powder
- 8 chicken drumsticks

Directions:

1. First of all, please make sure you've all the ingredients available. Put together salt, five spice powder, pepper, & sand ginger in a mixing bowl.
2. Now put Roll chicken drumsticks on the mixture until evenly coated.
3. Wrap chicken with parchment paper.

4. This step is important. Place in a large size container & then pour water.
5. Then place the trivet into the Instant Pot Pressure Cooker.
6. Lock the lid in place. Press the high pressure & cook properly for about 15 to 20 minutes.
7. Now when the beep sounds, Choose Natural Pressure Release. Depressurizing would take 20 to 25 minutes.
8. One thing remains to be done. Turn off the Instant Pot. Remove the lid.
9. Finally adjust seasoning according to your preference. Serve.

Serves: 4 to 6

Recommended Serving Size: 1-2 drumsticks

Yeah, it is a vintage recipe.

Nutritional information:

Calories – 31

Carbohydrates – 0 gram

Fat – 0 gram

Protein – 6 grams

Yummy Italian Chicken Marsala
Always the upper hand...

Ingredients:

- Salt and pepper to taste
- 1/2 cup chicken stock
- 1/4 cup potato starch
- About 1 teaspoon herbes de provence
- 3 tablespoons olive oil
- 2 tablespoons butter
- About 2.5 onions (Chopped)
- 1 cup dry marsala wine
- 3 cloves of garlic (Minced)
- 1-pound cremini mushrooms (Sliced)
- 2 chicken breasts, bones, and skin removed

Directions:

1. First of all, please make sure you've all the ingredients available. Season the chicken with salt and pepper. Dredge into potato starch. Set aside.
2. Now press the Sauté button on the Instant Pot. Heat olive oil.
3. Place the dredged chicken pieces & allow to brown lightly for about 2 to 5 minutes on each side. Set aside.
4. This step is important. Place the butter & sauté the onions and garlic until fragrant.
5. Then quickly add the rest of the ingredients & place the chicken.
6. Season with more salt & pepper to taste.
7. Now close the lid & press the Poultry button.
8. One thing remains to be done. Adjust the cooking time to about 15 to 20 minutes.

9. Finally do natural pressure release.

Serves: 4 to 5

Preparation Time: 5 to 10 minutes

Cooking Time: 15 to 20 minutes

Now you're happy…?

Nutritional information:

Calories per serving:207

Carbohydrates: 25.5g

Protein: 11.6g

Fat:8.3g

Fiber:3.8g

Unique Beef And Broccoli

Classic style…

Ingredients:

- 1 1/2 cup broccoli florets
- Salt
- About 1 1/2 tbsp cornstarch
- 2 garlic cloves (Minced)

- Pepper
- 2 1/2 tbsp brown sugar
- About 1 tbsp sesame oil
- 1/2 onion (Sliced)
- 1/4 cup soy sauce
- 1/2 cup beef broth
- 0.75 lb beef chuck roast, sliced into strips

Directions:

1. First of all, please make sure you've all the ingredients available. Now please use the "Slow Cooker" setting on your Instant Pot.
2. Now add beef & onion into the slow cooker.
3. In a bowl, mix together broth, garlic, sesame oil, brown sugar, and soy sauce. Season with pepper and salt.
4. This step is important. Pour mixture over beef.
5. Cover and cook properly on low for about 2.5 hours or until meat has cooked.
6. Then ladle out little broth from slow cooker & pour into the bowl.
7. Add cornstarch and whisk until smooth. Return broth & cornstarch mixture into the slow cooker and stir gently.
8. Now add broccoli florets to the slow cooker.
9. One thing remains to be done. Cover and cook properly for about 10 to 15 minutes or until broccoli is tender.
10. Finally serve & enjoy.

Total Time: 2 hours 20 to 25 minutes

Serves: 2 to 4

Arrive in style with this recipe.

Nutritional information:

Calories 775

Fat 51.4 g

Carbohydrates 26.4 g

Sugar 14 g

Protein 50.1 g

Cholesterol 175 mg

Ultimate Very Tender Pot Roast

Ironic in taste…

Ingredients:

- 4 potatoes; large-sized, cut into large cubes
- 4 carrots (Chopped)
- 2 stalks celery (Chopped)
- About 3.5 tbsp steak sauce; optional
- 3 cloves garlic
- 1 onion
- 2 tbsp Italian Seasonings
- 1 cups beef broth
- 1 cup red wine
- 2 to 3 pounds beef; chuck roast
- 2 tbsp olive oil

Directions:

1. First of all, please make sure you've all the ingredients available. Press the "Sauté" key of your Instant Pot. Pour in the olive oil.
2. Then add the roast beef & cook each side for about 2 minutes or until browned.
3. Transfer the browned beef into a plate.
4. This step is important. Put the celery, carrots & potatoes in the pot.
5. Now top with the garlic & onion.
6. Pour the beef broth & the wine in the pot.
7. Next, quickly put the roast on top of the vegetables.
8. Then spread the seasonings over the top of the roast & then spread with the steak sauce.
9. Press the "Cancel" key to stop the sauté function. Cover & lock the lid.
10. Now press the "Manual" key; set the pressure to "High"; and set the timer for about 35 to 40 minutes.
11. When the Instant Pot timer beeps; release the pressure naturally for about 10 to 15 minutes or until the valve drops.
12. One thing remains to be done. Turn the steam valve to release remaining pressure.
13. Finally unlock & carefully open the lid. Serve!

Servings: 6 to 7

Prep + Cook Time: 50 to 55 minutes

Looking forward to this one!!

Nutritional information:

Calories:- 499

Fat:- 15.9

Fiber:- 4.9

Carbs:- 30.4

Protein:- 49.8

Iconic Chicken Avocado Soup

Used to eat this one a lot.

Ingredients:

- 3 garlic cloves (Minced)
- About 1.5 onion (Diced)
- 1 lime, freshly squeezed
- 1 can chopped tomatoes
- 1 can black beans
- 1/2 jalapeno pepper (Diced)
- 3 chicken breasts, large dices
- 1/2 cup cilantro (Chopped)
- 5 cups chicken broth
- 1 cup corn
- About 1 tsp. paprika
- 1 tsp. cumin
- 1/2 cup avocado (Diced)
- 1 tsp. oregano

- Pinch of salt
- 1 tbsp. olive oil
- Pinch of pepper

Directions:

1. First of all, please make sure you've all the ingredients available. Pour olive oil into the crockpot. Press the "saute" button.
2. Now sauté garlic & onion for about 2 to 5 minutes or until tender and aromatic.
3. Cook tomatoes, black beans, chicken breasts, jalapeno pepper, chicken broth, cumin, corn, paprika, oregano, salt, and pepper.
4. This step is important. Lock the lid in place.
5. Then press the high pressure and cook properly for about 10 tto 15 minutes.
6. When the beep sounds, Choose the Quick Pressure Release.
7. This will depressurize for about 5 to 10 minutes. Remove the lid.
8. One thing remains to be done. Turn off the crockpot. Adjust seasoning according to your preferred taste.
9. Finally to serve, put cilantro, avocado dices, & lime juice on top.

Serves: 4 to 5

Recommended Serving Size: 11/2 cups

There it is.

Nutritional information:

Calories – 109.2

Carbohydrates – 7.6 grams

Fat – 9 grams

Protein – 1.7 grams

Beef, Lamb, Turkey And Pork

Awesome Sunday Brussels Sprouts.

Leave a mark!!

Ingredients:

- 5 slices bacon (Chopped)
- Pepper; to taste
- About 1/2 tsp. salt
- 1/4 cup. soft goat cheese; optional
- 2 tbsp. balsamic reduction
- 6 cups. Brussels sprouts (Chopped)
- About 2.5 tbsp. water

Directions:

1. First of all, please make sure you've all the ingredients available. Press the "Sauté" key of the Instant Pot.
2. Now add the bacon & sauté until desired crispiness is achieved.
3. This step is important. Add the Brussels sprouts & stir to coat with the scrumptious bacon fat.

4. Add the water and sprinkle with pepper and salt.
5. Then cook for about 2 to 5 minutes, stirring occasionally & continue sautéing until the Brussel sprouts are crisp.
6. One thing remains to be done. Transfer into a serving dish.
7. Finally drizzle with balsamic reduction & if desired, sprinkle with crumbled goat cheese.

Servings: 6 to 8

Prep + Cook Time: 35 to 40 minutes

Spice up!!

Nutritional information:

Calories:- 140

Fat:- 8.1

Fiber:- 3.3

Carbs:- 8.4

Protein:- 9.9

Super Beef Mushroom Stroganoff

What do you think? ?

Ingredients:

- 11/2 tablespoons oil
- 3/4 cup sour cream
- About 1 tablespoons garlic

- 11/2 teaspoons black pepper
- 3/4 cup diced onions
- 1 cup water
- About 1 teaspoons salt
- 2 cups mushroom, chopped
- 11/2 lbs beef stew meat

Directions:

1. First of all, please make sure you've all the ingredients available. Select the 'sauté' function on the instant pot.
2. Then add the oil. the onions & garlic. Cook properly for about 2 to 5 minutes.
3. This step is important. Add the remaining ingredients, except the sour cream.
4. Secure the lid and set the cooker on 'manual' for about 20 to 25 minutes at high pressure.
5. One thing remains to be done. Now after the beep, 'natural release' the steam and remove the lid after 20 to 25 minutes.
6. Finally stir in the sour cream & serve.

Serves: 6 to 8

Prep time: 5 to 10 minutes

Cooking time: 35 to 40 minutes

What makes this the best? Check it out for yourself!!

Nutritional information:

Calories: 317

Carbohydrate: 4.4g

Protein: 36.4g

Fat: 16.6g

Sugar: 1.1g

Sodium: 675mg

Delightful Pork Tender In Tropical Sauce

Just got better!!

Ingredients:

- 1/2 cup tomato puree
- 2 cloves
- 1 cup unsweetened pineapple juice
- About 1 teaspoon cinnamon
- 1/2 cup pineapple chunks
- 1/2 teaspoon nutmeg
- 1/4 cup chopped onion
- About 1 teaspoon rosemary
- 1/2 lbs. pork tenderloin

Directions:

1. First of all, please make sure you've all the ingredients available. Heat up the Instant Pot then select "Sauté" menu.
2. Now cut the pork into slices then place in the Instant Pot.

3. Add tomato puree & pineapple juice to the pot then sprinkle chopped onion, cloves, rosemary, nutmeg, & cinnamon on top.
4. This step is important. Cover the Instant Pot with the lid then make sure that it is locked properly.
5. Then select "Manual" setting then cook the pork properly on high for about 25 to 30 minutes.
6. Quickly release the Instant Pot then open the lid.
7. One thing remains to be done. Add pineapple chunks to the pot then stir well. Do not need to reheat it again.
8. Finally transfer to a serving dish then enjoy warm.

Serves: 2 to 4

Preparation time: 5 to 10 minutes

Cooking time: 25 to 30 minutes

Got the idea!!

Nutritional information:

Calories: 291

Total Fat: 5g

Saturated Fat: 1.7g

Protein: 31.7g

Carbs: 30.7g

Fiber: 3.6g

Sugar: 20.4g

Fantastic Mouthwatering Garlic Meatballs

Relax and enjoy this recipe!!

Ingredients:

- Spinach1 cup
- Bone brothas required
- Garlic1/4 cup
- Large carrot4.5
- Salt and pepperto taste
- Ground beef1 lb.

Directions:

1. First of all, please make sure you've all the ingredients available. Chop the carrot into 1/2 inch chunks.
2. Now add the chunks & the bone broth to an instant pot.
3. This step is important. In a medium or large mixing bowl mix the beef with pepper, salt, garlic, and spinach & then roll up into convenient size meatballs.
4. Then arrange the meatballs on the carrots chunks.
5. One thing remains to be done. Close the lid and manually set the time for about 15 to 20 minutes at high pressure.
6. Finally when the cooking is done, release the pressure & serve immediately.

Overall cooking time: 45 to 50 min

Servings: 4 to 5

Try this one if you're hungry!!

Nutritional information:

Calories: 192

Fat: 11g

Carbs: 3g

Protein: 32g

Sodium: 0.06g.

Great Garlic Spicy Sausage Meal

Make me remember the good old days!!

Ingredients:

- 4 minced cloves
- 10 pieces of Italian Sausage
- 1 (15 ounces) can tomato sauce
- 1 (28 ounces) can diced tomatoes
- About 3 to 4 large green bell peppers, seeded, cored and make small chunks
- About 1.5 tablespoon basil
- 1 cup water
- About 1.5 tablespoon Italian seasoning

Directions:

1. First of all, please make sure you've all the ingredients available. Place your Instant Pot on a flat kitchen surface; plug it & turn it on.
2. Now open the lid, and one by one add the tomatoes, basil, tomato sauce, garlic powder, Italian seasoning and water in the pot.
3. Add the sausage and pepper; do not mix. Carefully close its lid & firmly lock it.
4. This step is important. Then after, seal the valve too.
5. Then to start making the recipe, press "Manual" button.
6. You have to set cooking time; set the timer for about 25 to 30 minutes.
7. Allow the pot to cook the mixture until the timer goes off.
8. Now turn off the pot & press "Cancel."
9. Allow the built up pressure to vent out naturally; it will take 5 to 10 minutes to completely release inside pressure.
10. One thing remains to be done. Open its lid and transfer the cooked mixture into serving container/containers.
11. Finally serve warm!

Prep Time: 5 to 10 min.

Cooking Time: 25 to 30 min.

Number of Servings: 5 to 6

Luxury in its own class!!

Nutritional information:

Calories - 317

Fat – 21g

Carbohydrates – 17g

Fiber – 5g

Protein – 18.6g

Mighty Collard With Bacon.

Healthy is a new trend these days!! ? Always I guess…

Ingredients:

- About 1 tsp. kosher salt
- 1/2 cup. water
- 1 lb. collard greens; cleaned and then stems trimmed
- Fresh ground black pepper
- 1/4 lb. bacon; cut into 1-inch pieces

Directions:

1. First of all, please make sure you've all the ingredients available. Now quickly spread the bacon in the bottom of the Instant Pot inner pot.
2. Now press the "Sauté" button & cook properly for about 5 to 10 minutes, occasionally stirring until the bacon is crispy & browned.
3. Stir in a big handful of collard greens to coat with bacon grease until slightly wilted. Pack in the rest of the collards.
4. This step is important. The pot will be filled –just pack them enough to close the lid since they will quickly wilt.

5. Then sprinkle the greens with salt & pour water over everything. Close and lock the lid.
6. Turn the steam release valve to "Sealing", set the pressure to "High"; and the timer to about 20 to 25 minutes.
7. Now when the timer beeps; turn the steam valve to "Venting" to quick release the pressure. Carefully open and remove the lid.
8. One thing remains to be done. Pour the collard into a serving dish.
9. Finally sprinkle with freshly ground black pepper & then serve.

Servings: 6 to 7

Prep + Cook Time: 40 to 45 minutes

Stunner!!

Nutritional information:

Calories:- 123

Fat:- 8.4

Fiber:- 2.5

Carbs:- 4.4

Protein:- 8.7

Pinnacle Homemade Spaghetti Squash And Meat Sauce
Super awesome plus unique!!

Ingredients:

- Onion 1 small
- Cheese for topping
- Garlic cloves 3
- Kosher salt 1.5 tbsp.
- Black pepper to taste
- Spaghetti squash 1 large
- Tomatoes 8, crushed.
- Ground beef 1 lb.
- Bay leafs required

Directions:

1. First of all, please make sure you've all the ingredients available. Place the beef in the pot & add the garlic, salt, pepper, and onion.
2. Now set the cooker to sauté for about 5 to 10 minutes.
3. This step is important. Add the crushed bay leaf, tomatoes, and cheese then stir.
4. Take the spaghetti squash & pierce with a knife and place over the sauce.
5. Then close the lid and cook properly for about 15 to 20 minutes.
6. One thing remains to be done. When cooled, cut the spaghetti squash in half & scoop out the strands.
7. Finally serve squash with sauce & cheese.

Overall cooking time: 30 to 35 min

Servings: 5 to 7

Iconic recipe of my list!!

Nutritional information:

Calories: 341

Fat: 12g

Carbs: 17g

Protein: 24g

Sodium: 672mg

Dashing Eastern Lamb Stew

Well it is a Grandma's recipe!!

Ingredients:

- 1 (1/2 -13/4) lb lamb stew meat
- 1/2 cup raisins (Chopped)
- About 2.5 onions, diced
- 8 garlic cloves (Chopped)
- 2 teaspoons salt
- 2 (15 oz.) cans chickpeas, rinsed and drained
- 2 teaspoons pepper
- 2 teaspoons cumin
- About 2.5 teaspoons coriander
- 21/2 cups chicken broth
- 2 teaspoons turmeric,
- 4 tablespoons honey or brown sugar

- 2 teaspoons cinnamon
- About 1.5 teaspoon chilli flakes
- 4 tablespoons tomato paste
- 1/2 cup apple cider vinegar
- 4 tablespoons olive oil

Directions:

1. First of all, please make sure you've all the ingredients available. Select the 'sauté' function on the instant pot.
2. Now add the oil, garlic & all the spices. Sauté for about 2 to 5 minutes.
3. Stir in all the remaining ingredients and secure the lid.
4. Then switch the cooker to the 'meat stew' mode for 1 hour 15 to 20 minutes.
5. One thing remains to be done. After the beep, 'natural release' the steam & remove the lid.
6. Finally stir the stew and serve with fresh cilantro on top.

Serves: 8 to 9

Prep time: 15 to 20 minutes

Cooking time: 1 hour 20 to 25 minutes

Happiness has finally arrived!!

Nutritional information:

Calories: 1010

Carbohydrate: 87.2g

Protein: 65.4g

Fat: 44.2g

Sugar: 27.9g

Sodium: 1018mg

Charming Tasty Sausage Soup

Whenever you want a great recipe!!

Ingredients:

- 2 cups kale (Chopped)
- About 1/2 tsp salt
- 2 potatoes, cubed
- 1 carrot (Grated)
- 1/4 tsp red pepper flakes
- 1/4 cup heavy cream
- 1/2 lb Italian sausage, browned
- 2 3/4 cups chicken broth

Directions:

1. First of all, please make sure you've all the ingredients available. Now please use the "Slow Cooker" setting on your Instant Pot.
2. Then add all ingredients to the slow cooker & stir well.
3. One thing remains to be done. Cover and cook properly on low for about 3 to 4 hours.

4. Finally stir well & serve.

Total Time: 4 hours 10 to 15 minutes

Serves: 2 to 3

How is it? Only one way to find out…

Nutritional information:

Calories 682

Fat 39.8 g

Carbohydrates 45.3 g

Sugar 5 g

Protein 34.9 g

Cholesterol 116 mg

Perfect Corned Beef

I can eat them all day!!

Ingredients:

- Red potatoes 20
- Cornstarch 2 tbsp. (for gravy)
- Onion 1.5 medium
- Garlic cloves
- Spice packet 1
- Beef broth 4 cups.

- Corned beef brisket 2 1/2 lbs.
- Cabbage 1 head

Directions:

1. First of all, please make sure you've all the ingredients available. Place the beef into the instant pot, add the potatoes, garlic, onion and pour the broth over everything.
2. Then sprinkle the spices over the whole arrangement.
3. Close the lid & set the time to about 40 to 45 minutes at low pressure.
4. This step is important. After cooking, remove the lid and cool.
5. Add the cabbage and cook again properly for about 10 to 15 minutes.
6. Now remove the meat but not the drippings.
7. One thing remains to be done. Add 2 tbsp. cornstarch with the drippings.
8. Finally blend & cook until boiling. Lower the temperature & thicken slowly.

Overall cooking time: 55 to 60 min

Servings: 6 to 7

Different take on this one…

Nutritional information:

Calories: 228

Fat: 16g

Carbs: 3g

Protein: 16g

Sodium: 1g

Pinnacle Savory Instant Salsa Pork

Take a small break from your daily life and just try making something different for once. You never know what you may find but we can always give it a shot.

Ingredients:

- 2 garlic cloves (minced)
- Pepper and salt as needed
- 1 cup green salsa
- 1 pound pork, make small chunks
- About 1.5 teaspoon cumin
- 1 onion (Diced)

Directions:

1. First of all, please make sure you've all the ingredients available. Place your Instant Pot on a flat kitchen surface; plug it & turn it on.
2. Now to start making the recipe, press "Sauté" button.
3. Add the pork, onion, and garlic; cook properly for a few minutes to soften the ingredients.
4. This step is important. Mix the cumin & salsa. Carefully close its lid and firmly lock it. Then after, seal the valve too.

5. Then to start making the recipe, press "Meat/Stew" button.
6. You have to set cooking time; set the timer for about 30 to 35 minutes.
7. Allow the pot to cook the mixture until the timer goes off.
8. Now turn off the pot & press "Cancel."
9. Allow the built up pressure to vent out naturally; it will take 5 to 10 minutes to completely release inside pressure.
10. One thing remains to be done. Open its lid & transfer the cooked mixture into serving container/containers.
11. Finally serve warm over rice with your favorite vegetables.

Prep Time: 5 to 10 min.

Cooking Time: 30 to 35 min.

Number of Servings: 4 to 5

Yeah, you can make it in your free time…

Nutritional information:

Calories - 206

Fat – 13g

Carbohydrates – 16.2g

Fiber – 0g

Protein – 7.3g

Crazy Italian Lamb Shanks.

I am interested!!

Ingredients:

- 3 carrots; peeled and chopped
- 4 cloves garlic; minced Italian parsley, chopped, for garnish
- 1 can (14 oz.) fire-roasted tomatoes
- About 1.5 yellow onion (Diced)
- 1 tbsp. tomato paste
- 3 stalks celery (Diced)
- 1 tbsp. coconut oil
- 1 tbsp. balsamic vinegar
- About 1 tsp. crushed red pepper flakes
- 1 cup. beef stock
- 1/4 tsp. pepper
- 1/2 tsp. salt
- 3 lb. lamb shanks

Directions:

1. First of all, please make sure you've all the ingredients available. Sprinkle the lamb shanks with pepper & salt.
2. Now press the "Sauté" key of the Instant Pot & wait until hot.
3. Add the coconut oil and heat.
4. When the oil hot; cook the lamb shanks for about 5 to 10 or until all sides are browned. Transfer into a platter.
5. This step is important. Add the onion, garlic, celery and carrots in the pot.
6. Then season with pepper & salt.
7. Cook, frequently stirring, until the onion is somewhat translucent - be careful not to burn the garlic.

8. Now add the fire-roasted tomatoes & the tomato paste. Stir to mix. Return the lamb shanks in the pot.
9. Add the beef stock & balsamic vinegar.
10. Press the "Cancel" key to stop the sauté function.
11. Then cover & lock the lid.
12. Press the "Manual" key; set the pressure to "High"; and set the timer for about 45 to 50 minutes.
13. When the Instant Pot timer beeps; release the pressure naturally for 10-15 minutes or until the valve drops.
14. Now turn the steam valve to release remaining pressure. Unlock & carefully open the lid.
15. One thing remains to be done. Transfer the lamb shanks in a serving plate. Ladle the sauce over the shanks.
16. Finally garnish with chopped fresh parsley.

Servings: 4 to 5

Prep + Cook Time: 1 hour 10 to 15 minutes

Good days!!

Nutritional information:

Calories:- 405

Fat:- 28.8

Fiber:- 3.4

Carbs:- 13.3

Protein:- 98.3

King Sized Korean Beef

Now that's something!!

Ingredients:

- Lean beef 1 lb.
- Green onion 1, sliced
- Garlic 1 clove
- Brown sugar 1/4 cup
- Red pepper 1/2 tsp.
- Sodium soy sauce 1/4 cup
- Sesame oil 2 tbsp.
- Ground ginger 1/2 tsp.

Directions:

1. First of all, please make sure you've all the ingredients available. Set the instant pot's temperature to sauté and add the sesame oil.
2. Now add the beef with garlic and cook properly for about 45 to 50 minutes.
3. Add the ground ginger, soy sauce, red pepper and sugar. Combine well.
4. One thing remains to be done. Then quickly close the lid and manually set the time to about 5 to 10 minutes at high pressure.
5. Finally after cooking, release the pressure & serve hot.

Overall cooking time: 45 to 50 min

Servings: 4 to 6

Can you make it? Yes, why not?

Nutritional information:

Calories: 280

Fat: 13g

Carbs: 15g

Protein: 23g

Sodium: 0.6g

Mighty Garlic Beef Sirloin

Life of a legend begins here.

Ingredients:

- About 4.5 teaspoons garlic powder
- Salt and pepper to taste
- 8 cloves garlic, minced
- 6 lbs beef top sirloin steak
- 1 cup butter

Directions:

1. First of all, please make sure you've all the ingredients available. Select the 'sauté' function on the instant pot.
2. Now pour in the oil & add the sirloin steaks.
3. This step is important. Cook properly for about 5 to 10 minutes. Let the meat brown on each side.

4. Stir in all the remaining ingredients & secure the lid.
5. Then switch the cooker to the 'meat stew' mode & cook properly for about 30 to 35 minutes.
6. One thing remains to be done. After the beep, 'natural release' the steam & remove the lid.
7. Finally serve hot.

Serves: 8 to 9

Prep time: 10 to 15 minutes

Cooking time: 50 to 55 minutes

Funny but definitely yummy!!

Nutritional information:

Calories: 865

Carbohydrate: 2g

Protein: 103.9g

Fat: 44.3g

Sugar: 0.4g

Sodium: 368g

Nostalgic Pineapple Pork

Something is definitely different.

Ingredients:

- 1 tsp fish sauce
- 1 tsp salt
- About 1.5 tsp olive oil
- 1/2 cup pineapple (Diced)
- About 1.5 tsp liquid smoke
- 2 lbs pork shoulder, cut into 2 pieces
- 1/2 cup water

Directions:

1. First of all, please make sure you've all the ingredients available. Add olive oil into the instant pot & select sauté mode of the instant pot.
2. Now sear pork each half for about 2 to 5 minutes on each side until lightly brown.
3. This step is important. Season pork with salt.
4. Add pork, fish sauce, pineapple, liquid smoke & water to the pot.
5. Then seal pot with lid & cook on the manual setting for about 85 to 90 minutes.
6. Allow releasing pressure naturally then open the lid.
7. One thing remains to be done. Remove pork from instant pot & using forks shred the meat.
8. Finally serve and enjoy.

Serves: 8 to 9

Preparation time: 10 to 15 minutes

Cooking time: 90 to 95 minutes

This is epic. Take a look!!

Nutritional information:

Calories: 342

Total Fat: 24.9g

Saturated Fat: 9g

Protein: 26.5g

Carbs: 1.4g

Fiber: 0.1g

Sugar: 1.1g

Meatless Cuisines, Ketogenic, Main Dish

Tasty Berry Sauce In Minutes

Wow, just wow!!

Ingredients:

- 2 cups blueberries, reserve some for garnish
- 1/2 cup walnuts crumbled, freshly toasted, for garnish
- 2 cups raspberries, reserve some for garnish

- 1 cup water
- 1/2 cup dried coconut shavings, for garnish
- 1/2 cup brown sugar
- About 1.5 tsp. lemon juice, freshly squeezed
- 1 piece vanilla bean, halved lengthwise
- 2 cups strawberries, reserve some for garnish

Directions:

1. First of all, please make sure you've all the ingredients available. Place strawberries, blueberries, water, raspberries, brown sugar, and vanilla bean into the Instant Pot Pressure Cooker.
2. Now lock the lid in place. Press the high pressure & cook properly for about 10 to 15 minutes.
3. This step is important. When the beep sounds, Choose the Quick Pressure Release.
4. This will depressurize for about 5 to 10 minutes. Remove the lid.
5. Then discard spent vanilla bean. Stir in lemon juice.
6. Adjust seasoning according to your preferred taste.
7. Transfer to an immersion blender. Puree until smooth. Chill.
8. One thing remains to be done. To serve, pour chilled fruit sauce on top of fresh berries.
9. Finally garnish with crumbled walnuts & coconut shavings.

Recommended Serving Size: 1/4 cup

Show time!!

Nutritional information:

Calories – 20.6

Carbohydrates – 5.4 grams

Fat – 0 grams

Protein – 0.3 grams

Yummy Corned Beef

For those who are not ordinary, try this one.

Ingredients:

- 2 oranges (Sliced)
- 17 ounces water
- About 2.5 garlic cloves (Minced)
- Salt and black pepper to the taste
- 2 yellow onions, thinly sliced
- 11 ounces celery, thinly sliced
- 4 cinnamon sticks, cut into halves
- About 1.5 tablespoon dill, dried
- 3 bay leaves
- 4 pounds beef brisket

Directions:

1. First of all, please make sure you've all the ingredients available. Put the beef in a bowl, add some water to cover,

leave aside to soak for a few hours, drain & transfer to your instant pot.
2. Then add celery, orange slices, bay leaves, onions, garlic, dill, cinnamon, pepper, dill, salt, & 17 ounces water.
3. One thing remains to be done. Stir, cover the pot and cook properly at High for about 45 to 50 minutes.
4. Finally transfer meat to a cutting board, slice, divide among plates, drizzle the juice & veggies from the pot over beef & serve. Enjoy!

Preparation time: 10 to 15 minutes

Cooking time: 60 to 65 minutes

Servings: 5 to 6

Be amazed ?

Nutritional information:

Calories 251

Fat 3.14

Fiber 0

Carbs 1

Protein 7

Unique Mustard Spinach Instant Meal

Cooking level infinite....

Ingredients:

- 2-inch knob ginger (Minced)
- Pinch of dried fenugreek leaves
- 2 onions, diced
- About 1.5 teaspoon garam masala
- 1 teaspoon cumin
- 1 pound spinach, rinsed
- 1 teaspoon coriander
- 1/2 teaspoon black pepper
- About 1 teaspoon cayenne
- 1 pound mustard leaves, rinsed
- 1/2 teaspoon turmeric
- 2 teaspoons salt
- 2 tablespoons ghee
- 4 garlic cloves (Minced)

Directions:

1. First of all, please make sure you've all the ingredients available. Place your Instant Pot on a flat kitchen surface; plug it & turn it on.
2. Now to start making the recipe, press "Sauté" button. \Add the ghee, garlic, spices, and onions; cook properly for about 2 to 5 minutes to soften the ingredients.
3. Add the spinach and stir; cook until turn wilted.
4. This step is important. Now add the mustard greens & carefully close its lid and firmly lock it. Then after, seal the valve too.

5. Then to start making the recipe, press "Manual" button. Now you have to set cooking time; set the timer for about 15 to 20 minutes.
6. Allow the pot to cook the mixture until the timer goes off.
7. Turn off the pot & press "Cancel."
8. Now allow the built up pressure to vent out naturally; it will take 5 to 10 minutes to completely release inside pressure.
9. One thing remains to be done. Open its lid & transfer the cooked mixture into serving container/containers.
10. Finally serve warm with bread!

Prep Time: 5 to 10 min.

Cooking Time: 15 to 20 min.

Number of Servings: 5 to 6

Uber fantastic!!

Nutritional information:

Calories – 80

Fat – 5g

Carbohydrates – 6g

Fiber – 3g

Protein – 4g

Ultimate Braised Green And Red Cabbage

Deserved!!

Ingredients:

- 1 1/2 lbs. red cabbage, sliced into wedges 1 cup water
- 1/2 tsp. salt
- 1/4 cup mushroom stock
- About 2.5 Tbsp. coconut oil
- 1/2 cup carrots, grated
- 1/8 tsp. roasted sesame oil
- 1/2 tsp. red pepper flakes
- 1/4 cup coconut vinegar
- 1/4 cup fresh parsley tops, torn
- About 1.5 tsp. brown sugar
- 2 lbs. green cabbage, sliced into wedges
- About 1 tsp. cayenne powder

Cornstarch slurry

- About 2.5 tsp. cornstarch dissolved in…
- 2 Tbsp. water

Directions:

1. First of all, please make sure you've all the ingredients available. Press the "saute" button. Pour olive oil into the Instant Pot Pressure Cooker.
2. Now cook cabbage wedges until partially cooked.
3. Transfer to a holding plate.

4. This step is important. Repeat the same cooking procedure until all cabbages are cooked.
5. Then add in mushroom stock, red pepper flakes, carrots, coconut vinegar, brown sugar, and cayenne powder into the crockpot.
6. Lock the lid in place. Press the high pressure & cook properly for about 5 to 10 minutes.
7. Now when the beep sounds, Choose the Quick Pressure Release.
8. This will depressurize for about 5 to 10 minutes.
9. Remove the lid. Arrange vegetables on a serving dish.
10. For the gravy, press the "saute" button.
11. Then stir in cornstarch slurry. Cook until gravy thickens.
12. Add in sesame oil and salt. Adjust seasoning according to your preferred taste.
13. One thing remains to be done. To serve, place just the right amount of cooked veggies on plates. Put some gravy on top of the veggies.
14. Finally garnish with fresh parsley.

Serves: 4 to 6

Recommended Serving Size: 11/2 cups

Long way to go…

Nutritional information:

Calories – 108

Carbohydrates – 14.24 grams

Fat – 5.07 grams

Protein – 1.77 grams

Iconic Beef Bourguignon

The speed matters…

Ingredients:

- 2 carrots (Sliced)
- Salt and black pepper to the taste
- 1/2 cup beef stock
- 1 cup dry red wine
- About 1/2 teaspoon basil, dried
- 3 bacon slices (Chopped)
- 8 ounces mushrooms, cut into quarters
- 2 garlic cloves (Minced)
- About 2.5 tablespoons white flour
- 12 pearl onions
- 10 pounds round steak, cubed

Directions:

1. First of all, please make sure you've all the ingredients available. Set your instant pot on Sauté mode, add bacon & brown it for 2 minutes.
2. Then add beef & flour, stir and brown for about 5 to 10 minutes.

3. One thing remains to be done. Add salt, pepper, wine, stock, onions, garlic and basil, stir, cover and cook on High for 20 minutes.
4. Finally add mushrooms & carrots, cover the pot again, cook properly on High for about 5 to 10 minutes more, divide everything between plates and serve. Enjoy!

Preparation time: 15 to 20 minutes

Cooking time: 30 to 35 minutes

Servings: 6 to 8

Be super

Nutritional information:

Calories 442

Fat 17.2

Fiber 3

Carbs 16

Protein 39

Awesome Sweet Potato Cauliflower
Being lucky is definitely better.

Ingredients:

- 1 (15 ounces) can diced tomatoes

- 1 onion, peeled and chopped
- About 1.5 tablespoon peanut butter
- 1/4 teaspoon cayenne pepper
- 1/2 teaspoon cumin seeds
- 1 teaspoon salt
- 1 (15 ounces) can chickpeas, rinsed and drained
- 3 cloves garlic (Minced)
- About 1.5 tablespoon mild curry powder, divided
- 1 pound sweet potatoes peeled and cubed
- 1 large head cauliflower, make small flowerets
- 4 cups vegetable broth
- 1/8 teaspoon cinnamon
- 1 small chili pepper, seeded and minced
- About 1.5 tablespoon ginger paste
- 3-4 cups water

Directions:

1. First of all, please make sure you've all the ingredients available. Place your Instant Pot on a flat kitchen surface; plug it & turn it on.
2. Now to start making the recipe, press "Sauté" button.
3. Add the oil and onions; cook properly for about 2 to 5 minutes to soften the ingredients.
4. Add the cumin seeds, garlic, chili pepper and ginger & cook properly for about 30 to 40 seconds; stir in between.
5. This step is important. Add the cinnamon, broth, potatoes and 1 teaspoon curry powder and carefully close its lid & firmly lock it.
6. Now after, seal the valve too.

7. To start making the recipe, press "Manual" button.
8. You have to set cooking time; set the timer for about 2 to 5 minutes.
9. Then allow the pot to cook the mixture properly until the timer goes off.
10. Turn off the pot and press "Cancel." Allow the built up pressure to vent out naturally; it will take 5 to 10 minutes to completely release inside pressure.
11. Now open its lid and press "Sauté" button
12. One thing remains to be done. Add the cauliflower, 3 cups of water, chickpeas, tomatoes, cayenne pepper, 2 teaspoons curry powder & salt; simply cook the mixture until the cauliflower is tender.
13. Finally mix in the peanut butter & serve warm!

Prep Time: 5 to 10 min.

Cooking Time: 10 to 15 min.

Number of Servings: 7 to 8

Mystery is unveiled!!

Nutritional information:

Calories – 319

Fat – 4g

Carbohydrates – 53.2g

Fiber – 18g

Protein – 17.7g

Super Spinach And Edamame Stew

If you're a legend, then make this one.

Ingredients:

- 2 cups shelled edamame, frozen
- 1/4 cup chives, minced, for garnish
- About 1.5 Tbsp. chili oil
- Pinch of black pepper
- 4 cups mushroom stock
- 1/2 cup mozzarella cheese, shredded
- About 1.5 Tbsp. soy sauce
- 2 tsp. sesame oil
- 4 cups baby spinach leaves

Directions:

1. First of all, please make sure you've all the ingredients available. Pour sesame oil, edamame, black pepper, chili oil, mushroom stock, and soy sauce into the Instant Pot Pressure Cooker.
2. Now lock the lid in place. Press the high pressure & cook properly for about 5 to 10 minutes.
3. This step is important. When the beep sounds, Choose the Quick Pressure Release.
4. This will depressurize for about 5 to 10 minutes. Remove the lid.
5. Then turn off the machine.
6. Add in mozzarella cheese & baby spinach.

7. One thing remains to be done. Adjust seasoning according to your preferred taste.
8. Finally to serve, ladle soup into bowls. Garnish with chives.

Serves: 3 to 4

Recommended Serving Size: 1 plate

Nutritional information:

Calories – 152

Carbohydrates – 13.9 grams

Fat – 4.6 grams

Protein – 12.1 grams

Something is special!!

Delightful Cauliflower Soup

Stupidly simple...

Ingredients:

- 1 small yellow onion (Chopped)
- 1/2 cup coconut milk
- 1 cauliflower head, florets separated and chopped
- 3 cups chicken stock

- About 1.5 teaspoon garlic powder
- 1 cup cheddar cheese (Shredded)
- 4 ounces cream cheese, cubed
- About 2.5 tablespoons olive oil
- A pinch of salt and black pepper

Directions:

1. First of all, please make sure you've all the ingredients available. Set your instant pot on sauté mode, add oil, heat it up, add onion, stir and cook properly for about 2 to 5 minutes.
2. Now add cauliflower, stir and cook properly for about 2 minutes more.
3. Add stock, mil and garlic powder, stir, cover & cook properly on High for about 5 to 10 minutes.
4. One thing remains to be done. Then add cream cheese & pulse everything using an immersion blender.
5. Finally add cheddar cheese, stir soup, ladle into bowls & serve. Enjoy!

Preparation time: 10 to 15 minutes

Cooking time: 10 to 15 minutes

Servings: 4 to 6

Be unique, be extraordinary…

Nutritional information:

Calories 261

Fat 4

Fiber 4

Carbs 7

Protein 8

Fantastic Quinoa Mixed Vegetable

Just make it once and you will keep making it!!

Ingredients:

- About 2.5 tablespoons rice vinegar
- 8-ounce bag mixed vegetables, frozen
- 1 thumb grated ginger
- 4 cups water
- About 2.5 tablespoons of sugar
- 2 cups quinoa
- 2 tablespoons soy sauce

Directions:

1. First of all, please make sure you've all the ingredients available. Place your Instant Pot on a flat kitchen surface; plug it & turn it on.
2. Now open the lid, & one by one add the mentioned ingredients in the pot except for veggies.
3. This step is important. Carefully close its lid and firmly lock it. Then after, seal the valve too.
4. To start making the recipe, press "Manual" button.

5. Then you have to set cooking time; set the timer for about 2 minutes.
6. Allow the pot to cook the mixture properly until the timer goes off.
7. Now turn off the pot & press "Cancel."
8. One thing remains to be done. Allow the built up pressure to vent out naturally; it will take 5 to 10 minutes to completely release inside pressure.
9. Finally open its lid & add in the vegetables; serve warm!

Prep Time: 5 to 10 min.

Cooking Time: 2 to 5 min.

Number of Servings: 2 to 3

I've always loved them. Plus they can be eaten anytime!!

Nutritional information:

Calories - 456

Fat – 7g

Carbohydrates – 42.3g

Fiber – 9.2g

Protein – 18g

Great Zucchini Noodles In Tomato Soup

The hit list recipe.

Ingredients:

For the zucchini

- Pinch of salt
- 4 zucchini, processed into thin ribbons using a spiralizer
- Pinch of black pepper

For the stew

- 1 cup onion (Diced)
- About 1/4 cup flat leaf parsley, chopped, for garnish
- About 2.5 Tbsp. garlic, grated
- 1 tsp. sweet paprika powder
- 1 tsp. red pepper flakes
- 1 can tomatoes (Diced)
- 1 cup green pitted olives
- 1 cup kale leaves, julienned
- About 1/2 tsp. thyme powder
- Pinch of salt
- 1/2 cup red wine
- Pinch of black pepper
- 3 cups vegetable stock
- 2 Tbsp. olive oil

Directions:

1. First of all, please make sure you've all the ingredients available. Put together zucchini noodles, salt, & pepper in a colander. Set aside to drain.
2. Now to make the stew, pour olive oil into the Instant Pot Pressure Cooker. Press the "saute" button.
3. Saute garlic and onion for about 2 to 5 minutes or until limp and translucent.
4. This step is important. Add in tomatoes, olives, vegetable stock, thyme powder, red wine, sweet paprika powder, and red pepper flakes.
5. Then season with salt and pepper.
6. Lock the lid in place. Press the manual button & cook properly for about 5 to 10 minutes.
7. When the beep sounds, Choose Natural Pressure Release. Depressurizing would take 20 to 25 minutes.
8. Now remove the lid. Turn off the machine. Tip in kale leaves.
9. One thing remains to be done. To serve, place just the right amount of zoodles on a plate.
10. Finally pour stew on top. Garnish with parsley.

Serves: 3 to 4

Recommended Serving Size: 3/4 cup

Some things never fail you.

Nutritional information:

Calories – 93.8

Carbohydrates – 11.5 grams

Fat – 4.8 grams

Protein – 2.2

Happy Chicken And Delicious Sauce

Mushroom fries bring back a lot of memories.

Ingredients:

- About 1.5 tablespoon lemon juice
- A pinch of salt and black pepper
- 1 cup Greek yogurt
- About 1/2 teaspoon ginger, grated
- 1 tablespoon garam masala
- 2 chicken breasts, skinless, boneless and chopped

For the sauce:

- 4 garlic cloves, minced
- About 1/2 teaspoon cayenne
- 15 ounces canned tomato sauce
- 1/2 teaspoon turmeric
- About 1 teaspoon paprika
- 4 teaspoons garam masala

Directions:

1. First of all, please make sure you've all the ingredients available. In a bowl, mix chicken with lemon juice, yogurt, ginger, 1 tablespoon garam masala, salt and pepper, toss well & leave aside in the fridge for 1 hour.
2. Now set your instant pot on sauté mode, add chicken, stir & cook properly for about 5 to 10 minutes.
3. One thing remains to be done. Then add 4 teaspoons garam masala, tomato sauce, garlic, paprika, turmeric and cayenne, stir, cover the pot & cook properly on High for about 10 to 15 minutes.
4. Finally divide between plates & serve. Enjoy!

Preparation time: 1 hour and 10 to 15 minutes

Cooking time: 20 to 25 minutes

Servings: 4 to 6

My sister makes it every now & then.

Nutritional information:

Calories 452

Fat 4

Fiber 7

Carbs 9

Protein 12

Lucky Broccoli Chickpea

For a eternal experience.

Ingredients:

- 1 (15 ounces) can chickpeas, drained
- About 1 teaspoon olive oil
- Crushed red pepper as needed
- 3 large cloves of garlic (Chopped)
- About 1/4 teaspoon fennel seeds
- 1 bunch broccoli rabe, halved
- Salt as needed
- 1/4 cup vegetable broth

Directions:

1. First of all, please make sure you've all the ingredients available. Place your Instant Pot on a flat kitchen surface; plug it & turn it on.
2. Now to start making the recipe, press "Sauté" button.
3. Add the oil and garlic; cook properly for about 2 to 5 minutes to brown the garlic.
4. This step is important. Add the seeds and red pepper; cook properly for about 30 to 35 seconds.
5. After, add the broth, broccoli, & chickpeas.
6. Then carefully close its lid and firmly lock it. Then after, seal the valve too.
7. To start making the recipe, press "Manual" button.
8. You have to set cooking time; set the timer for about 2 to 5 minutes.

9. Allow the pot to cook the mixture properly until the timer goes off.
10. Now turn off the pot and press "Cancel."
11. Allow the built up pressure to vent out naturally; it will take 5 to 10 minutes to completely release inside pressure.
12. One thing remains to be done. Open its lid & transfer the cooked mixture into serving container/containers.
13. Finally serve warm!

Prep Time: 5 to 10 min.

Cooking Time: 10 to 15 min.

Number of Servings: 3 to 4

Like never before…

Nutritional information:

Calories - 506

Fat – 10g

Carbohydrates – 44.3g

Fiber – 12g

Protein – 24.3g

Vintage Chicken Macaroni Salad – Limit This Dish To Once A Week Worth it…

Ingredients:

- 1 lb. elbow macaroni, cooked al dente

For the chicken

- 1 1/2 cups chicken thigh fillets
- 11/2 cups vegetable stock
- Pinch of salt

For the dressing

- 1 cup mayonnaise
- Pinch of white pepper
- 3/4 cup raisins
- 1/2 cup celery, minced
- 3/4 cup carrots, grated
- 1 can crushed pineapple, drained

Directions:

1. First of all, please make sure you've all the ingredients available. For the chicken, combine chicken fillets, vegetable stock, and salt into the Instant Pot Pressure Cooker.
2. Now lock the lid in place. Press the high pressure & cook properly for about 25 to 30 minutes
3. This step is important. When the beep sounds, Choose the Quick Pressure Release.
4. This will depressurize for about 5 to 10 minutes.

5. Then remove the lid. Turn off the machine.
6. Shred chicken. Put together pasta, chicken, & cooking liquid in a bowl.
7. To make the salad, fold chicken pasta mix with celery, pineapple, carrots, mayonnaise, raisins, & pepper.
8. One thing remains to be done. Adjust seasoning according to your preferred taste.
9. Finally cover with saran wrap. Place inside the fridge for about 1.5 hour or until ready to serve.

Serves: 2 to 4

Recommended Serving Size: 1 cup salad – limit this

Nutritional information:

Calories – 438.8

Carbohydrates – 30.2 grams

Fat – 22.6 grams

Protein – 11.3

Simple recipe for you…

Best Green Olives Instant Potatoes
For those who're ultra fantastic.

Ingredients:

- 1 1/2 cup diced carrots

- 4 cups potatoes, make bite-sized pieces
- 2 cups water
- 1 cup green peas
- 1 cup corn kernel

Make dressing:

- 1/4 cup + 1 tablespoon mayo
- About 1 teaspoon salt
- 1/2 teaspoon ground black pepper
- 10 green olives, minced

Directions:

1. First of all, please make sure you've all the ingredients available. Place your Instant Pot on a flat kitchen surface; plug it & turn it on.
2. Now open the lid, and one by one add the carrots, potatoes, and water in the pot.
3. Carefully close its lid & firmly lock it.
4. This step is important. Then after, seal the valve too.
5. To start making the recipe, press "Manual" button. Now you have to set cooking time; set the timer for about 10 to 15 minutes.
6. Then allow the pot to cook the mixture until the timer goes off.
7. Turn off the pot & press "Cancel."
8. Allow the built up pressure to vent out naturally; it will take 5 to 10 minutes to completely release inside pressure.
9. Now open its lid & transfer the mixture to a separate bowl.

10. In the empty pot, add the corn and peas; close the lid. Press "Manual" button.
11. You have to set cooking time; set the timer for about 2 minutes.
12. One thing remains to be done. Transfer the cooked mixture into serving container/containers.
13. Finally mix the dressing ingredients & potato mixture, and mix well. Serve warm!

Prep Time: 5 to 10 min.

Cooking Time: 15 to 20 min.

Number of Servings: 6 to 7

Simple yet tasty recipe.

Nutritional information:

Calories – 295

Fat – 9g

Carbohydrates – 45.2g

Fiber – 6g

Protein – 6.3g

Nostalgic Different Lasagna

Wizard of all recipes.

Ingredients:

- 1 pound beef, ground
- 8 ounces mozzarella, sliced
- About 1.5 yellow onion (Chopped)
- 1 egg
- 20 ounces keto marinara sauce
- 1/2 cup parmesan cheese, grated
- 1 and 1/2 cups ricotta cheese
- About 2.5 garlic cloves, minced

Directions:

1. First of all, please make sure you've all the ingredients available. Set your instant pot on sauté mode, add onion, garlic & beef, stir and sauté for about 5 to 10 minutes.
2. Now add marinara sauce, stir & transfer half of this mix to a bowl. In another bowl, mix ricotta with parmesan & egg and whisk well.
3. This step is important. Add half of the mozzarella to your instant pot & spread.
4. Then add half of the ricotta mix & spread.
5. Add the remaining beef and marinara mix, the rest of the mozzarella & the rest of the ricotta mix.
6. One thing remains to be done. Cover this with some tin foil, cover the pot & cook properly on High for about 10 to 15 minutes.
7. Finally slice lasagna, divide between plates & serve. Enjoy!

Preparation time: 10 to 15 minutes

Cooking time: 25 to 30 minutes

Servings: 8 to 9

Another fantastic recipe for you guys…

Nutritional information:

Calories 339

Fat 4

Fiber 2

Carbs 8

Protein 36

Mighty Walnut Beet Lunch Bowl

Magical taste.

Ingredients:

- 1 1/2 pounds beets, scrubbed, rinsed
- 2 cups water

Dressing:

- 1 teaspoon Dijon mustard
- Pepper and salt as needed
- About 2.5 teaspoons apple cider vinegar
- 1 1/2 tablespoons olive oil, extra virgin
- 1 1/2 teaspoons sugar

- About 2.5 teaspoons lemon juice
- 2 tablespoons walnuts (Chopped)

Directions:

1. First of all, please make sure you've all the ingredients available. Place your Instant Pot on a flat kitchen surface; plug it & turn it on.
2. Now open the lid, and one by one add the water and beets in the pot. Carefully close its lid & firmly lock it.
3. Then after, seal the valve too.
4. To start making the recipe, press "Manual" button.
5. This step is important. Now you have to set cooking time; set the timer for about 10 to 15 minutes.
6. Then allow the pot to cook the mixture until the timer goes off.
7. Turn off the pot & press "Cancel."
8. Allow the built up pressure to vent out naturally; it will take 5 to 10 minutes to completely release inside pressure.
9. Now open its lid & transfer the cooked mixture into a bowl.
10. Drain the beets and chop into bite-sized pieces.
11. In a mixing bowl; add all the ingredients for the dressing except oil and walnuts.
12. One thing remains to be done. Whisk to combine thoroughly & add the olive oil slowly into the dressing; combine well.
13. Finally add the dressing over the beets, toss & serve!

Prep Time: 5 to 10 min.

Cooking Time: 2 to 5 min.

Number of Servings: 2 to 3

Vintage overload…

Nutritional information:

Calories – 151

Fat – 10g

Carbohydrates – 15.2g

Fiber – 3g

Protein – 2.7g

Thanks for reading my book.

Printed in Great Britain
by Amazon